Breakthrough: Women in Archaeology

Barbara Williams

Foreword by H. M. Wormington

Walker and Company
New York

Library of Congress Cataloging in Publication Data

Williams, Barbara. (Breakthrough)
Women in archaeology.

Index included.
SUMMARY: Biographies of six successful women archaeologists. Includes information on making archaeology a career and lists archaeological field schools, departments of anthropology/archaeology, and museum departments.
1. Women archaeologists—Juvenile literature.
2. Archaeology—Vocational guidance—Juvenile literature.
[1. Women archaeologists. 2. Archaeologists.
3. Archaeology—Vocational guidance. 4. Vocational guidance] I. Title. II. Series: Breakthrough (New York)
CC110.W54 1981 930.1'092'2 [B] 80-7687
ISBN 0-8027-6406-1

FIRST PUBLISHED IN THE UNITED STATES OF AMERICA IN 1981 BY THE WALKER PUBLISHING COMPANY, INC.

PUBLISHED SIMULTANEOUSLY IN CANADA BY BEAVERBOOKS, LIMITED, DON MILLS, ONTARIO.

DESIGNED BY DAVID NETTLES

ISBN: 0-8027-6406-1

LIBRARY OF CONGRESS CATALOG CARD NUMBER: 80-7687

PRINTED IN THE UNITED STATES OF AMERICA

10 9 8 7 6 5 4 3 2 1

Contents

Foreword by H. M. Wormington		*v*
Introduction		*viii*
Chapter 1	*Cynthia Irwin-Williams*	*1*
Chapter 2	*Jane Holden Kelley*	*25*
Chapter 3	*Karen Olsen Bruhns*	*51*
Chapter 4	*Leslie E. Wildesen*	*73*
Chapter 5	*Ernestene Green*	*91*
Chapter 6	*Mary Eubanks Dunn*	*113*
Glossary		*128*
Appendix 1	*Archaeological Field Schools*	*131*
Appendix 2	*Departments of Anthropology/ Archaeology*	*149*
Appendix 3	*Museum Departments*	*166*
Index		*169*

FOREWORD

IT WOULD BE IMPOSSIBLE to say that prejudice against women in archaeology has ceased to exist, but it has diminished to such a remarkable extent that it is difficult to believe how strong it was even a few decades ago. In the late 1930s I can remember meeting only a very few colleagues who were women, but they included some outstanding individuals: Dorothy Cross who worked in the eastern United States; Marjorie Lambert, Clara Lee Tanner and Bertha Dutton, who were southwestern specialists. Attending professional meetings, one now finds that a large percentage of the archaeologists present are women. There has also been a dramatic increase in the number of women who have held high offices in professional archaeological societies.

Some of the early prejudices held by many, though by no means all, male archaeologists stemmed from the belief that women could not withstand the rigors of the field. Later activities by many archaeologists, who are women, have amply demonstrated that this is not the case.

It was also feared by some that marriage, and probably children, would make it impossible for a wife and mother to be an archaeologist. It is true that some promising careers have come to an end because of these factors; but, as this book demonstrates so clearly, the problems of combining a career with marriage and motherhood are not insurmountable.

Problems do exist, of course, and much depends on the attitude of the man whom an archaeologist marries. In my own case, I feel the deepest gratitude to my husband, George D. Volk, who died in February 1980, only a few months before we were to have celebrated our fortieth wedding anniversary. His keen interest in my career and warm supportive attitude enabled me to undertake a wide range of activities, some of which involved long periods of separation.

One problem that must be emphasized is discussed in the Introduction—the scarcity of jobs in universities and museums, and the ever increasing number of candidates for every position that becomes available. The fact that certain universities with few women on their faculties are making some effort to increase their numbers is good. However, both men and women with Ph.D.'s far exceed the number of positions that are available.

In the Anthropology Newsletter of the American Anthropological Association published in January 1980, there was an excellent discussion of "Ph.D.'s in Non-Academic Careers: Are There Good Jobs?" by Lewis C. Solmon. It stressed the serious decline in academic job opportunities but concluded that "few doctorate holders are unemployed for long. Markets adjust. People adjust. And there are good jobs available outside academe."

It is indeed fortunate that in recent years there has been increasing emphasis on the preservation of prehistoric and historic sites, for there are many more jobs for administrators in federal and state organizations than there were in the past. Also, some archaeologists have been quite successful in establishing themselves as contract archaeologists who evaluate and, in some cases, excavate sites that are threatened by other activities and that must be salvaged to conform with federal and state regulations. In view of this possible option, it would seem desirable for those planning for a career in archaeology to seek to obtain some training in business administration.

It should be stressed that no matter what type of job an archaeologist hopes to obtain, field experience is absolutely necessary. Even an archaeologist who is an administrator and who may not be actively conducting studies in the field must understand the problems involved.

As this book makes clear, the path to a career in archaeology is a long and grueling one. It also shows with equal clarity that it is possible to achieve this goal. For those who persevere, archaeology can produce an exciting and richly rewarding life, one characterized by constant intellectual stimulus, interesting colleagues, and, in some cases, extensive travel and the opportunity to study different life ways of contemporary people as well as those of the prehistoric past.

H. M. WORMINGTON

INTRODUCTION

BY THE TIME British archaeologist Margaret Murray had worked up her courage to attend a conference with her male colleagues, she was fifty years old. As far as she knew, no other woman had ever ventured into a meeting of the British Association of Anthropology, but when Dr. Murray arrived for the morning session in Birmingham, England in 1913, she discovered another woman hiding timidly behind a pile of books and sitting as far away from the men as possible. Murray, however, boldly took a seat among the men, smoking with them and contributing to the discussion by angrily suggesting that the wives of diplomats—as well as the diplomats themselves—should be educated in advance about the customs of the countries where they were to be stationed.

Before the afternoon session of the conference began, a man Dr. Murray knew rather well took the seat beside her and told her sorrowfully that he did not approve of the statements she had made in the morning, or even of her presence at the conference. "There are many things in this world a woman shouldn't know," he said. "I certainly would not permit you to attend one of my lectures."

In those days prior to Freud, Kinsey, Masters and Johnson, and X-rated movies, Western women were presumed to have little interest in sex and were "protected" from information about a subject men thought women would find shocking. Since fertility rites were at the core of many ancient religions and since anthropologists spend a good deal of time investigating sexual practices in primitive societies, the discipline's subject matter itself was one reason most men tried to exclude women from the study of anthropology in the late nineteenth and early twentieth centuries.

Anthropology is a broad science that deals with the origin, development, and customs of the various peoples of the world. College students can major in anthropology for their bachelor's degrees, but that training won't prepare them for any specific career. If they want to become professional anthropologists, they must go on to graduate school to obtain their master's and/or doctor's degrees in one of the four fields of specialization within anthropology: (1) linguistics, (2) physical anthropology, (3) ethnology, and (4) archaeology.

Linguistics, which is the science of language, is the least "controversial" of all the subfields of anthropology and therefore posed no particular threats historically as a subject for women to study. Dr. Margaret Murray, mentioned above, became an archaeologist by the roundabout manner of becoming a linguist first. Encouraged by her sister (who had wanted to do it herself until motherhood interfered), Murray began studying Egyptology at the University College in London under Sir Flinders Petrie in 1894. Eight years and several thousand hieroglyphs later, Petrie invited her to join his crew to excavate at Abydos in Egypt. Something of an eccentric for his time, Petrie engaged four other women for his crew in addition to his wife and Dr. Murray, in part because he felt that women were particularly good at illustrating artifacts and sites. Receiving such an auspicious start on a Petrie crew, Murray continued working on archaeological digs until all such excavating ceased during World War II. Although she never directed an excavation herself, she had a long career as a writer on archaeology, publishing one of her most famous books (*The Splendour That Was Egypt*) on her eighty-sixth birthday and her final two books in 1963—*when she was one hundred years old*!

Physical anthropology, which is the study of human evolution and the present races of the world, has been a controversial profession for men as well as for women because members of fundamentalist churches believe that the concept of human evolution contradicts the Bible's story of creation and have therefore tried to prevent evolution from being taught in public schools and state-supported universities. Presently, however, scientists refer to human evolution as a "principle" rather than a "theory," pointing among other things to the research in East Africa conducted by Mary Leakey and her late husband, Louis. Although technically an archaeologist and not a physical anthropologist, Mary Leakey has become identified with evolution by virtue of her most important find, a fossilized human skull nearly two million years old, which she excavated in 1959.

Ethnology (or cultural anthropology), which is the science that compares and analyzes cultures, was not a career easily accessible to women until about fifty years ago because of the sexual content of its research. Today her books seem like bland, mainstream investigations, but in 1928 Margaret Mead raised eyebrows when she published *Coming of Age in Samoa,* dealing with the behavior of adolescent girls in a permissive society. Dr. Mead's many subsequent books and her articles for popular magazines as well as for professional journals helped make her one of the most famous ethnologists in the world before she died in November 1978. Many other American women have also made noteworthy contributions to the study of ethnology, including Ruth Benedict, who taught at Columbia University before her death in 1948; Ruth Underhill, a former professor at the University of Denver; and Cora Du Bois, a former professor at Harvard University.

Archaeology, which is the study of a past people through the excavation and description of that people's material remains and environment, has been the most difficult of the four subfields of anthropology for women to penetrate. This is partly because male archaeologists long believed that women were not physically capable of digging in the hot sun, partly because the long skirts women once wore (and short skirts, too, for that matter) were not suitable for field work, and partly because most men (Flinders Petrie was a notable exception!) regarded any women save their wives as an encumbrance in the field. Not until affirmative action policies were implemented in the late 1960s did colleges and universities begin to hire women archaeologists in visible numbers. By that time, however, reduced college enrollments signaled a reduction in teaching positions for archaeologists of both sexes. The whole situation has caused one cynic to quip, "If women archaeologists ever had a fair chance, it lasted about five minutes."

Nevertheless, many women in the nineteenth century gained at least a certain kind of fame as archaeologists by marrying flamboyant males. Most notable among them was Sophia Schliemann, the beautiful wife of Heinrich Schliemann.

A multimillionaire who had acquired much of his wealth through war profiteering, Heinrich Schliemann was forty-seven years old in 1869 when he decided to divorce his first wife and find a younger one to help with his lifelong passion to find and excavate the lost city of Troy. Schliemann was a German by birth and an American by citizenship. His first wife was a Russian woman, who refused to leave her country, and Schliemann concluded he needed a Greek wife—a woman who could not only recite the famous passages of Homer but who was as beautiful as the legendary Helen.

In Indianapolis, Indiana, where he had paused briefly in his travels, Schliemann therefore filed for divorce against his wife in St. Petersburg and wrote to Archbishop Theoclitus Vimbos of Athens, who had formerly tutored him in Greek, petitioning the churchman's help in finding him a second wife, who was Greek, young, pretty, affectionate, and well-versed in classical mythology. The archbishop responded by sending photographs of several women, including one of his teenaged cousin, Sophia Engastromenos. From these photographs Schliemann selected Sophia as the woman he wanted to marry and promptly sailed to Greece so he could meet her. He made an unannounced visit to her school, listened to her recite Homer, fell madly in love, and married her within three weeks.

Schliemann himself was a self-taught scholar who eventually mastered twenty languages, becoming fluent in Turkish, for instance, within less than three weeks. Under his rigorous tutelage the seventeen-year-old schoolgirl who became his second wife was transformed into a sophisticated society woman in a few months. Heinrich also taught Sophia about foreign languages, art, music, theater, history, geography, philosophy, and archaeology while they waited for permission from the Turkish government to excavate the site at Hissarlik, where Troy, Schliemann believed, had once flourished.

Also while they waited, Sophia bore Heinrich the first of their children, but once the chance of excavating seemed hopeful,

Sophia left the child in Athens and accompanied Heinrich to Turkey. Together they excavated nine levels of civilization at Hissarlik (one level of which most scholars now agree was indeed the Troy that Homer had written about) and the civilization at Mycenae from which Agamemnon had sailed to Troy, uncovering, among other things, two golden diadems, sixty golden plates, six golden bracelets, sixty golden earrings, and 8,700 golden rings.

The story of the Schliemanns has so captivated the fancy of biographers and novelists that the couple has become the subject of numerous books and articles for children and adults. The best known of these many accounts is Irving Stone's fictionalized *The Greek Treasure*, published by Doubleday in 1976.

While the Schliemanns were excavating their classical treasures at sites near the Aegean Sea, a future woman archaeologist was growing up in America. Born in Boston in 1871, Harriet Ann Boyd Hawes graduated from Smith College in 1892 and subsequently undertook graduate work at the American School of Classical Studies in Athens. Deciding she was "not cut out for a library student," she implored the American School for an opportunity to assist with archaeological field research, but the school's faculty gave her no encouragement. She thereupon took the funds remaining in her fellowship and set off for the island of Crete, which she explored on muleback with another young woman from Boston; her male assistant, Aristides Pappadias; and Pappadias's mother (who went along to chaperone the young women). In the barren outskirts of Kavousi, in a region called Gournia, Hawes and Pappadias climbed a steep cliff, on the top of which they discovered and excavated an important Minoan site dating to the Bronze Age (about 1,000 B.C.). Hawes thus became the first woman archaeologist to lead an excavation in Crete and perhaps the first American woman to direct an excavation overseas. On later trips to Gournia in 1903 and 1904, this tiny woman of remarkable energy directed crews of more than one hundred male workers under conditions of extreme hardship.

When Harriet Hawes was ten years old, another future archaeologist, Hetty Goldman, was born, on December 19, 1881. In 1903 Goldman received her bachelor's degree from Bryn Mawr College in English, intending to become a novelist, but she abandoned that career as soon as she discovered she "had nothing to say." Instead, she registered for graduate courses in archaeology at Radcliffe and received her Ph.D. in 1916. Following in Hawes's footsteps, Goldman also became a fellow at the American School of Classical Studies in Greece and, no doubt, partially because of Hawes's accomplishments in Crete, was granted the privilege by the American School of becoming the first woman to lead an archaeological expedition under its auspices. After directing numerous other digs in Asia Minor, Yugoslavia, Greece, and Turkey (for the Fogg Museum at Harvard and for Bryn Mawr), she joined the Institute of Advanced Study at Princeton in 1936, retiring twenty years later on her seventy-fifth birthday. When she died on May 4, 1972, at the age of ninety, Dr. Goldman was widely acknowledged as a leading woman pioneer in archaeology.

A younger woman still active in the profession has achieved some pioneering honors of her own. She is H. Marie Wormington, an adjunct professor of anthropology at Colorado College in Colorado Springs and the author of several highly-regarded textbooks. Among these are *Ancient Man in North America*, which went into its fourth edition in 1957, and *Prehistoric Indians of the Southwest*, which went into a sixth printing in 1968. (Of the latter book Dr. Wormington now modestly admits, "It is hopelessly out of date, but some institutions still use it as a text. I wouldn't if I were teaching such a course, but nothing really adequate is available.")

Born in 1914 (the year after Margaret Murray was rebuked for attending the anthropology convention in Great Britain), Wormington received her B.A. degree from the University of Denver in 1935. She worked at the Denver Museum of Natural History for many years until she received a fellowship to attend graduate school at Radcliffe College in 1950. Arriving in Cambridge, Massachusetts, she discovered that most of the courses she needed for her Ph.D. specialty were offered through Harvard University rather than Radcliffe but that "some members of the department and some graduate students were less than enthusiastic about the admission of women." After cutting through considerable red tape, Wormington became the second woman admitted to study in the Harvard anthropology department and the first woman to specialize in archaeology in obtaining a Ph.D. from Harvard.

Several years later Dr. Wormington served two separate terms as the vice president of the Society for American Archaeology and was the first woman to be elected president of that organization in 1958. She is a member of Phi Beta Kappa and is listed in *American Men and Women of Science* and in *Who's Who of American Women*. Married to George D. Volk, a petroleum geologist, she retains her maiden name for professional purposes because she began publishing her well-known books and articles before she was married. The first edition of *Ancient Man in North America* came out in 1939, when she was only twenty-five years old and long before she attended graduate school at Harvard.

The careers of Harriet Boyd Hawes, Hetty Goldman, Marie Wormington, and even Mary Leakey dramatize the fact that women can no longer expect to become famous archaeologists simply by marrying men in the profession but must obtain solid educations in their own rights. Any high school student who hopes to become a professional archaeologist may want to write to one of the field schools listed on page 131 for information about summer training. Soon, however, she must start thinking very seriously about applying to one of the colleges listed on p. 149 to begin her four-year studies toward a B.A. degree in anthropology. Unless she is a serious student, more interested in education than in social activities, she may become discouraged because (1) she must maintain superior grades if she intends to go to graduate school (as all archaeologists must); (2) she should take courses in mathematics, computer science, chemistry, geology, botany, and foreign languages in addition to her anthropology requirements; (3) she may be expected to donate time on weekends to participate in salvage archaeology projects; and (4) she will probably spend her summers as a volunteer at some archaeological site. All of this means that it will be more difficult for her than it is for many other students to work her way through college. She should have money saved up now for college expenses or be prepared to borrow the necessary funds.

After obtaining her B.A. in anthropology from one institution a woman should enroll at a different university for her Ph.D. in the more specialized profession of archaeology. (Staying at the same school for all one's training is frowned upon because it limits a student's exposure to the varying points of view one can get by attending two or more schools.) While in graduate school a female student may experience subtle forms of sexual discrimination, discovering that the best teaching assistantships within her department go to male students or that on summer excavations the men get varied outdoor experience while women are shunted into laboratory work.

A prospective archaeologist will discover, if she perseveres and stays in graduate school despite the problems, that getting a Ph.D. degree (most archaeologists disdain their colleagues who quit school after obtaining only a master's degree) requires a minimum of three years beyond the B.A., during which time she must (1) continue to maintain excellent grades in her classes; (2) pass an oral examination in archaeology administered by five professors; and (3) write a paper (called a dissertation or thesis) of generally more than 150 pages documenting her original research in archaeology. Once these hurdles are passed, she will receive her doctorate, which is her credential as a qualified archaeologist.

Traditionally archaeologists have sought positions as college professors, spending their summers doing field work in various parts of the world. Three of the women whose biographies appear in this book (Cynthia Irwin-Williams in chapter 1; Jane Holden Kelley in chapter 2; and Karen Olsen Bruhns in chapter 3) pursue such careers and probably most archaeologists would like to do so. As indicated earlier, however, dwindling college enrollments in the 1970s and 1980s have resulted in fewer teaching positions, forcing recent Ph.D.'s to consider some of the other options within the archaeological profession.

One such option is to apply through the federal or state civil service register for an administrative position with the government as did two of the women whose biographies appear in this book (Leslie Wildesen in chapter 4 and Ernestene Green in chapter 5). Such a job will probably pay more at the outset than a job as an assistant professor at a university, but the former offers less upward mobility and far less opportunity to do field work in the summer. For a woman who is attracted to archaeology mainly because of its outdoor field work, government employment is usually dissatisfying. The exceptions to this rule are the jobs of ranger or of guide at a national monument that is also an archaeological site. At such places opportunities sometimes occur for people with other job descriptions to help with archaeological excavations. However, positions as rangers and guides do not pay very well and often are temporary jobs, for the summer seasons only.

Another possibility is to seek a career in museum work. Although some archaeologists scorn museum careers for the reason that so much time must be spent cataloging exhibits and answering mundane questions from the public, such recent innovations as the increase in outdoor exhibits are changing former attitudes. Furthermore, some museums are actively involved in archaeological research and foster a wide variety of programs. For more information about careers in museum work, high school and college students can write to one of the institutions listed on pages 166-168 for details about classes and internships in museology.

Still another option, especially suited to the unmarried professional who is willing to travel, is to become a free-lance archaeologist. Government-supported salvage archaeology programs have increased dramatically since World War II and because of recent legislation will continue in the federal budget for years to come. One of the women discussed in this book (Mary Eubanks Dunn in chapter 6) stays employed fairly steadily on a free-lance basis, but because of her marital status (she is the wife of a physician and has two small daughters), she cannot move about freely to locations where other work is available. Keeping abreast of projects also requires considerable imagination and time. but free-lancers can usually do so by writing to the anthropology departments in the various state universities. (See pages 149-165.)

For archaeologists interested in salvage projects in the states of Idaho, Montana, Oregon, Washington, and Wyoming, an interesting study entitled *Archaeological Handbook* was prepared in 1976 by Rick Pettigrew and Kimberly Shaw. Funded by the Western Interstate Commission for Higher Education (WICHE), this study is available in many public libraries or may be obtained by writing to the Bonneville Power Administration, Portland, Oregon. The study quotes the federal and state laws relating to salvage archaeology and lists the people responsible for coordinating projects in these five states.

Another study, much broader in its aims, was prepared by Charles R. McGimsey III, director of the Arkansas Archaeological Survey, and was published by the Seminar Press in 1972. Entitled *Public Archaeology*, this handbook gives helpful information about salvage archaeology throughout the fifty states, but since it was published before the enactment of important legislation regarding archaeology, the handbook is somewhat out of date.

Altogether, the image of the professional archaeologist is changing rapidly. The charming old British gentlemen (with or without their wives) dressed in khaki shorts and fanning themselves with jungle helmets while sipping afternoon tea no longer exist, and soon the college professors who teach archaeology nine months a year and excavate in exotic foreign countries for the remaining three months may be replaced by federal and state employees who travel about the United States to work on specific projects.

These changes are being effected partly by the new legislation concerning the preservation of historic and prehistoric sites and partly by new scientific techniques for interpreting sites and artifacts. But another factor, seldom appreciated by laymen, is that "there are simply no lost civilizations left to find" (see Brian M. Fagan, *Quest for the Past,* Addison-Wesley Publishing Company, Inc., 1978). This means that archaeologists of the future must be content to reinterpret sites that have already been excavated rather than actively seeking new digs. Such reinterpretation will require that they must be much more scientifically oriented than were the nineteenth-century excavators, like Heinrich Schliemann, Austen Henry Layard, Alexander Conze, and Augustus Pitt-Rivers, who established reputations as archaeologists mainly by the fact that they happened to dig at the right places at the right times.

All in all, the career problems for all archaeologists and the particular obstacles for women seem so challenging that one might wonder why any young person would choose to struggle seven years through college and graduate school. Yet all of the women whose biographies appear in this book faced serious challenges and most of them now find enormous satisfaction in what they are doing. Reading the stories of these six women may help young people to decide whether or not the enticements of a stimulating profession outweigh the many difficulties that exist in pursuing that profession.

Cynthia Irwin-Williams *Photo by Barbara Williams*

CHAPTER 1

CYNTHIA IRWIN-WILLIAMS

IF YOU TRAVEL through New Mexico by auto some weekend, you may encounter a small car burning up the highway between Albuquerque and Portales. Behind the wheel sits a robustly handsome woman who is more familiar with that particular stretch of land than the predatory birds that fly above it and she can outmaneuver drivers of the fastest sports cars. Dressed in her characteristic sleeveless white blouse and black beret—articles of clothing that have become her trademarks—she seems like a Parisian taxi driver whisking in and out of traffic around the Étoile. Actually she is Cynthia Irwin-Williams, recent president of the Society for American Archaeology, and the youngest person of either sex to hold that position.

Although archaeologists generally have a reputation for being slow and cautious, highway speed has become a way of life for Dr. Irwin-Williams. Like most women who try to pursue a career in archaeology, Cynthia Irwin-Williams has found it necessary over the years to make many trade-offs. One of her most difficult has been to commute nearly five hundred miles each weekend between her home in Albuquerque, where she lives four days a week with her husband, and her apartment in Portales, where she teaches three days a week at Eastern New Mexico University. Thus Dr. Irwin-Williams has learned to travel swiftly and, by her own admission (at least before OPEC sent American gasoline prices to three digits and maintaining the 55-MPH speed limit became a matter of national honor), she has developed the heaviest foot on the New Mexico interstate and the fanciest electronic equipment anywhere for intercepting radar patrols.

This life as a highway jockey began in 1963 when she and her husband, both newly armed with Ph.D's (hers from Harvard, his from M.I.T.), first presented themselves on the job market. Her husband, Dr. David Cary Williams, was trained as a nuclear chemist, a highly specialized profession that offers little mobility. The Sandia Corporation in Albuquerque, New Mexico, had an attractive opening for him on a government project, but no one in that city was interested in hiring a female archaeologist. In fact, the local state university was in the process of trying to lay off or to retire the only female anthropologists on its faculty. Cynthia looked around the state for employment for several months before she was finally reconciled to a dismal fact: If she wanted to work in the career for which she had been trained, she would have to take a part-time position 240 miles away in Portales, helping her friend Dr. George Agogino set up a new department in anthropology at Eastern New Mexico University.

The prospects of accepting a job so far away from her husband's posed at least three difficult problems: the expense of maintaining two different households, the time wasted in commuting back and forth each week, and the loneliness for both Cynthia and David in being separated so much. But Cynthia's mother tipped the scales in favor of Cynthia's accepting the job by volunteering to help. Mrs. Irwin offered to buy a home of her own in Albuquerque so the two women could drive back and forth each weekend, living together in an apartment in Portales on those days when Cynthia taught at the university. It seemed a very practical solution to Cynthia and Mrs. Irwin, who had worked as a team to overcome many previous obstacles that stood in the path of Cynthia's becoming an archaeologist.

David Williams, however, greeted the idea of sharing his bride with students so far away with something less than enthusiasm. Married less than a year, he was unprepared for the loneliness and increased responsibility that his wife's absences would mean. Emotionally he experienced great difficulty with the arrangement though he grudgingly realized there was no alternative. Cynthia had been preparing to become an archaeologist for nearly twenty years—since she was in grade school—and she wasn't the kind of woman to let a little thing like commuting five hundred miles each week interfere with her career.

Cynthia accepted the job at Eastern New Mexico University and for the next fifteen years worked with George Agogino to build the anthropology department there from a shoestring operation in 1963 to a very successful program, granting B.A. and M.A. degrees. Starting without exhibits or laboratories of any kind, the department eventually acquired three museums on various aspects of anthropology and a huge laboratory area, of four thousand square feet, which now houses some of the best equipment in New Mexico for analyzing pottery and stone tools and the only equipment in the state for analyzing prehistoric pollen. Meanwhile, Cynthia has personally contributed much to the science of archaeology through the excavations she has led, the papers she has delivered and published, and the professional offices she has held, including her recent one as president of the Society for American Archaeology.

All of Cynthia's professional activities were made considerably easier by the efforts of her mother, Eleanor C. Evans Irwin, who for the first ten years of Cynthia's professional life (from 1963 until Mrs. Irwin's death in 1973) spelled Cynthia off behind the wheel when they traveled back and forth between Albuquerque and Portales; cleaned and cooked in the Portales apartment; and even served as a confessor, handholder, and surrogate mother for Cynthia's students on summer field trips. Today Cynthia credits her mother with being the single most important person in her life, the goader and encourager who kept her on the track toward her career. "She was enormously strong, active, and limber clear up until the time of her death," Cynthia recalls. "And because of this she could participate in the archaeological work which we've done in New Mexico ever since we went there. She acted as the head of our archaeological reconnaissance operation from 1964 to 1970 and routinely outdistanced all my students who were about forty years younger."

On one occasion Cynthia sent her mother on a scouting operation with a vigorous young man who was training to run in a marathon race later in the fall. At the end of his day with Mrs. Irwin, he dragged into camp huffing and puffing. As he threw himself down in the shade he wailed, "That little old lady just walked my tail off!"

Like many other mothers who take fierce pride in their children's careers, Eleanor (Kay) Irwin was forced to give up her own dreams at an early age. Beginning in her youth as a very talented ballet dancer, she ultimately joined the famous troupe of Anna Pavlova, but just as success was looming she quit dancing to get married and then bore two children, Cynthia and Henry (both of whom were to grow up to become highly-regarded archaeologists). Not long after Henry was born, Kay Irwin divorced her husband, and as a young mother she had too many responsibilities at home to resume her dancing career.

In addition to the usual worries that young children give their mothers, Cynthia Irwin caused her mother real anguish, at least during her earliest years. Today Cynthia Irwin-Williams gives the impression that she was chiseled from granite, but she was born, on April 14, 1936, a spindly and asthmatic child who spent much of her first ten years in doctors' offices and in hospitals. Many were the nights Mrs. Irwin sat by Cynthia's bedside, taking turns at the vigil with Cynthia's grandfather, Henry F. Evans. "My mother and grandfather essentially kept me alive for the first nine or ten years of my life," Cynthia says gratefully.

These health problems, however, eventually led to an outdoor profession. "I was simply determined to overcome this disability which could easily have made me a semi-invalid," she explains. Instead, she developed her interest in sports, becoming the neighborhood tomboy, the recipient of several high school letters for track events and gymnastics, and eventually an energetic archaeologist.

With no father on the scene during her childhood, Cynthia looked to her grandfather for an academic, as well as athletic, role model. Henry Evans was one of those rare products of the nineteenth century, a wealthy businessman and scholar who was also completely self-made. Born in Maryland in 1862, he spent his early childhood amid the terror and deprivation of the Civil War. Because his Confederate family lost everything they owned in the war, after the armistice his father took up farming in a rural area of Kansas, where no schooling was available for his son. Henry Evans nevertheless determined to become an educated man and not only developed an exquisite command of the English language but also taught himself Latin, Greek, French, and German. In 1886 he moved with his new wife to Denver (where Cynthia was born much later), where he subsequently built up a very successful insurance business and established a local reputation as a scholar and historian. His genuine respect for learning was firmly established in his grandchildren, and though they were both under ten when he died in 1945, they never outgrew his impact on their lives.

After the death of this great old man, who had been such an imposing presence in the Irwin household, Mrs. Irwin became both father and mother to her children. There were financial problems, too, the thorniest of which was keeping Cynthia and her brother in the excellent private school where their grandfather had maintained them. Desperate to provide her children with a superior education, but unable to provide the tuition to the Graland School, Mrs. Irwin wondered if she couldn't volunteer her services to the school in exchange for keeping her children enrolled there. With a background as a ballet dancer and no professional credentials in education, Mrs. Irwin boldly applied for a job as a classroom teacher at Graland and persuaded the administration to hire her. For extra pocket money she snatched up all the odd jobs the administration offered—including driving the school bus.

Working at Graland gave Mrs. Irwin the chance to meet other teachers, and she developed fast friendships with some of them, particularly with Ruth Gorham, who taught sixth-and-seventh-grade history. Mrs. Gorham was deeply interested in American Indians and their history, and each year she and her family spent their summer living with Indian friends on the Hopi reservation in northern Arizona. The summer after Kay Irwin joined the faculty at Graland School, Ruth Gorham invited the Irwin family to vacation with hers, and for the next several years that pattern continued.

On the reservation the Gorham and Irwin children went on picnics with their young Hopi friends and played with them in both Indian and Anglo games. Some of their best times were those when they worked alongside the Hopi children in traditional Indian activities. They gathered yucca for basketry and clay for pottery and helped in the fields by picking such things as melons, corn, beans, and peaches. Although Cynthia and Henry were developing attitudes that would lead them to eventual careers in archaeology, at the time Cynthia realized only that she was "having a ball."

Much of this took place during or immediately after World War II, when adults all over the world were following the new reports with interest and concern. But there was very little grown-up conversation about kamikaze pilots and Nazi submarines on the Hopi reservation, where most of the Indians had little contact at that time with the outside world—no television sets and very few radios and newspapers. There was only a dirt track into the area where Cynthia stayed—not even a paved road to attract tourists—and the Indians grew the same crops, wore some of the same kinds of clothes, and worshipped the same gods as their ancestors had done hundreds of years earlier.

Besides the friends she made among the Hopi children, Cynthia became familiar with several adults in the Indian community. One of her good friends was Ned Lomayestewa, the head of the Antelope Religious Society in the village of Shungopovi. He had a little sheep ranch, where he permitted the children to look for arrow heads.

Their interest in arrow heads and other Indian artifacts continued after the school term had resumed and the Irwins had returned to Denver. On Sundays Mrs. Irwin would pack a picnic lunch and drive the children to some remote area where they could look for more arrow heads to add to their collections. This weekend activity was inexpensive, healthy, educational, and fun—an "idyllic" pastime, which cemented a happy family relationship. In time Mrs. Irwin and her two children joined the Colorado Archaeological Society, a Denver-based organization for amateurs that taught its members such things as what to look for in potsherds and how to comb through an area without disturbing any of those features that might be of genuine significance to a trained archaeologist. From the time she was in the fifth grade until she reached high school, Cynthia Irwin spent her weekends on amateur archaeological investigations, so that when her contemporaries were worrying if there would be enough snow to go skiing on Saturdays and Sundays, Cynthia would be worrying that there might be too much snow to go look for arrow heads and shards.

In high school Cynthia decided to organize some of her friends into an archaeology club and went about her task with a zeal that has characterized all her subsequent archaeological endeavors. After persuading her favorite teacher, Lawrence Marshall, to act as the club's official sponsor, she asked three highly regarded professionals (archaeologists H. Marie Wormington and Herbert Dick and anthropologist Ruth Underhill) to lend their services, too. They assisted by convincing qualified speakers to come to the club's monthly meetings and by providing slide shows and artifact displays. More importantly, Cynthia recalls, "they kind of acted as our unofficial godparents to make sure we didn't get into too much trouble by doing inadvertent damage to archaeological sites."

Weather permitting, on frequent weekends during the three years she served as the high school club president, Cynthia led her fellow students to prehistoric sites that she and her brother had located. Even in bad weather she could hold meetings at the school or write articles for the monthly archaeological newsletter that she and her best friends printed on an old-fashioned purple-inked ditto machine.

It was a period of her life that she recalls fondly—not only because of the good times—but also because she feels her efforts contributed to the science of archaeology in at least two ways: She modestly admits that she and the other high school students "did some pretty fair archaeology" on those weekend trips; she also thinks that her efforts encouraged several other young people to pursue archaeology as a career.

During those high school years Cynthia and Henry Irwin were also doing volunteer work for Marie Wormington at the Denver Museum of Natural History. Dr. Wormington gave them simple tasks at first—moving display cases, labeling artifacts, and making catalog listings—but she gradually assigned them more difficult responsibilities, like preparing indexes for her books. They also had an early opportunity of briefly going on one of Dr. Wormington's digs in western Colorado, an experience that left a lasting impression on both of them.

Although archaeology was Cynthia's main interest, she was a well-rounded student, who excelled in all academic subjects. In addition, she participated in sports and music, acted as a student assistant to history teacher Lawrence Marshall, and served as president of the astronomy club. Since by that time she had clearly decided to become a professional archaeologist, she sought Dr. Wormington's advice about which college to attend and ultimately sent off applications to Radcliffe and Bryn Mawr. As fortune would have it, Cynthia received scholarships to both colleges but decided on Radcliffe because of its association with Harvard University.

Adjacent to Harvard, Radcliffe in those days retained a partial autonomy. For those classes the administration thought should be segregated, such as gym, the women students remained isolated. But, in general, the female Radcliffe students sat alongside the male Harvard students in the same lecture halls. Thus it was in her freshman geology class in 1953 that Cynthia Irwin met David Williams. For their first date David invited her to accompany him to a laboratory demonstration on explosives given by a professor the students jokingly dubbed "the mad Russian." But the lecture proved to be more explosive than the romance. It took another nine years before the Irwin and Williams relationship got completely off the ground, and David and Cynthia were not married until September 1962. However, they made up for lost time by spending their honeymoon at a high elevation—climbing Long's Peak in Colorado's Rocky Mountain National Park.

Meanwhile—two years after Cynthia's admission to Radcliffe—her younger brother, Henry, was accepted at Harvard. All their lives the two Irwin children had maintained an intense sibling rivalry, competing with each other for better arrow heads, higher grades, and more interesting archaeological opportunities. But underneath the rivalry they were very proud of each other, and Cynthia was delighted to have her brother join her in Cambridge, Massachusetts.

Henry's acceptance at Harvard also meant that Kay Irwin could move to Cambridge to be with both of her children once again. The family was in serious financial straits (an unscrupulous real estate speculator had made off with most of Mrs. Irwin's inheritance from her father) and there was no way that both Irwin children could live in the East in separate dormitories. Kay Irwin therefore sold her home in Denver so she could buy a small home in Massachusetts and keep house for her two children while they attended college. She also worked as a teacher and babysitter to support her children while they were in school. When circumstances got really bad, she went out and did domestic work—cleaning floors, windows, walls, rugs. No honest work was too difficult or demeaning if it would help her children get a first-class education.

Early in her college education Cynthia discovered a fact of life that was to haunt her many times over: Women were not treated as equals in the archaeological profession. Throughout her high school years Cynthia had been a leader in amateur archaeological work, encouraging her friends to attend club meetings, taking them on weekend excavations, and teaching them all she knew. But now that she was attending a prestigious Eastern college and was well qualified to volunteer on someone else's archaeological crew, no one would give her a chance. She sent out literally hundreds of applications to archaeological projects and field schools, but most of them did not even bother to reply. Those that did said they were not willing to take a female on a field trip, even if she paid her own expenses.

Since members of the Irwin family do not give up easily, Cynthia, her mother, and her brother returned to Colorado during college vacations. For several summers the three Irwins excavated the LoDaiska site, a small rock shelter in the foothills of the Rockies outside Denver. They provided their own equipment and worked under the technical supervision of Marie Wormington. Eventually their labors resulted in a monograph published by the Denver Museum in 1959 that is still regarded as a classic in its field.

As for the sexual discrimination she suffered, Cynthia Irwin-Williams had the kind of fortitude that helped her overturn adversity. Recalling the early prejudice against her because she is a woman, she says, "It makes for a kind of 'do or die' point of view. The result for me was that I began to do individual independent research much earlier than people who found it easier to join large projects. Exclusion from the mainstream opportunities led to a fierce determination to do it on my own."

She did not land an assignment on a formal field project for several years. By then it was 1958, and she had received both her B.A. (magna cum laude) and M.A. degrees from Radcliffe and had been accepted into the Harvard program to start work on her Ph.D. degree in the fall. Because of the close association between

Radcliffe and Harvard, she had been working for several years as a laboratory assistant to a well-known Harvard professor. In the summer of 1958 he agreed to take her as a volunteer graduate student to a new dig he was starting in Europe. The dig's destination was a paleolithic site in southern France, where Cynthia hoped to begin work leading to her Ph.D dissertation in paleolithic archaeology.

Cynthia's first disappointment came when she saw the quarters in France where she would be living. Whereas the paid staff members lived in a respectable hotel, the student volunteers were assigned to dingy quarters above a fish shop and were told that they could not even visit the professional staff at the hotel. Furthermore, Cynthia discovered that as a woman she was expected to do the secretarial duties, leg work, and menial tasks that had very little to do with the study of archaeology.

"It was a very unhappy situation for everyone," she recalls, "and the only thing I can say about it is that I learned more about how *not* to run a project than anything else that summer. Immediately after that I began doing my own work, and I have not worked for anyone else since then. So my experience on other people's expeditions was brief and disappointing. But I suppose it reflects the tenor of the fifties and sixties."

One more-or-less legendary celebration that now occurs each summer on Irwin-Williams's excavations was born of her 1958 experience. The director of the 1958 dig reasoned there should be no Fourth of July celebration because his crew was working in France. In a peculiar Catch-22 reversal, he likewise reasoned that there should be no celebration of Bastille Day (the French national holiday on July 14) because his crew members were Americans. Cynthia swore solemnly to herself that when she became a project director, *both* holidays would be *thoroughly* celebrated. Hence every year, somewhere in the western United States, Bastille Day is marked by a huge (sometimes as many as 250 participants) dance and a barbecue that lights up the sky for miles around.

For a long time Cynthia was bitter about the discrimination she experienced and admits that she may have been too suspicious and hostile. But in the long run she has probably become a better archaeologist. She has bent over backwards trying to be fair with members of her crews, and she has learned how to survive in a tough society.

After it became clear that she would be a "permanent stooge" if she continued to study at Harvard under the professor with whom she had worked in Europe, Cynthia changed her field of specialization to New World archaeology and found a different sponsor in J. O. Brew, who at that time was director of Harvard's Peabody Museum. "Dr. Brew," she says warmly, "was an enormously generous person who bailed out a number of other students too and gave them their starts. He supported both my brother and me consistently in our careers at Harvard and gave us every opportunity to develop ourselves." Among other things, Dr. Brew helped provide a small grant which supported Cynthia's investigations at Magic Mountain in Colorado, studies that would later become the basis for her doctoral dissertation.

Meanwhile, Cynthia was nagged by several memories of discrimination and to rid herself of problems and to reassure herself that archaeology was really the career she wanted, she took off a year from graduate classes at Harvard in 1959 and embarked upon the most "madcap" experience of her life. Only twenty-two years old, skimpily funded, and unfamiliar with Spanish, she departed for Mexico to conduct archaeological excavations completely on her own.

As a mature archaeologist Dr. Irwin-Williams looks back in horror at that foolhardy decision. Recalling it, she shakes her head in disbelief and rolls her eyes toward the clouds. "Someone should have stopped me," she intones. As a matter of fact, several people did try to talk her out of it, but her mother, who always encouraged Cynthia and Henry to develop their talents, was not one of them. So Cynthia set off for some truly dangerous experiences south of the border. Fortunately, her year in Mexico also proved to be exhilarating and rewarding.

The decision to go to Mexico was the outgrowth of Cynthia's chronic need to discover "new things"—some subject in the New World on which relatively little research had already been done. Deciding to focus on the postpaleo and preceramic cultures of the Indians of central Mexico (the period after they used stone tools but had not yet learned to make pottery), she obtained a small, predoctoral grant of $133 a month from the National Science Foundation. Her first month's paycheck was ample enough to buy a one-way ticket to Mexico City but didn't leave her much to live on the rest of the month. Thus she ate very little while she gamely tried to pick up enough Spanish words and phrases to acquaint herself with archaeological data at the National University of Mexico and the National Institute of Anthropology.

One of the first people she met in Mexico was a student named Braulio Garcia, an Indian from an area just south of Mexico City who had been befriended by Mormon missionaries and had joined their faith. He spoke a brand of Spanish that Cynthia later learned was "perfectly frightful," but for long periods at a stretch he was the only person to whom she ever talked. Pleased with her gradual ability to communicate with him, Cynthia didn't realize until much later that she was learning a kind of Spanish that would put her at a disadvantage when she tried to converse with Mexican college professors and archaeologists.

Hearing of Cynthia's grant from the National Science Foundation, Braulio agreed to serve as her guide and assistant through the Mexican backcountry, where she hoped to find a site to research. Although she knew it was risky to go off to rural areas with a comparative stranger, Cynthia had no choice but to trust the young Indian. As things turned out, she had little reason to worry about Braulio's character—only about his recklessness and stupidity behind the wheel of an automobile.

Before they could travel to the back country, however, Cynthia had to obtain a vehicle with four-wheel drive. Unable to find anything suitable in Mexico City, she and Braulio made their way across the border to San Antonio, Texas, where Cynthia mortgaged sixty dollars a month of her future National Science Foundation paychecks for an ancient jeep.

Riding beside Braulio in the jeep, Cynthia spent the next six months exploring for sites in Mexico, testing them, and deciding on which ones to excavate. She was looking for a cave or rock shelter that showed evidence of a sequence of "archaic" cultures. Weeks turned into months as Cynthia and Braulio continued their bumpy reconnaissance. Then, suddenly, her activities were halted by a frightening experience.

Braulio had been driving the jeep along a lonely stretch of road in his usual imprudent manner when he hit a bad bump and the jeep rolled over and over and over—three times. Cynthia was not hurt, but the jeep was so badly damaged that it was knocked out of commission for some time. More importantly, Braulio sustained serious injuries. Cynthia had to administer first aid and comfort for twelve hours before the police finally arrived. Meanwhile, of course, she sat by the side of the road wondering if help would ever come.

When help did come, after making certain that Braulio would be all right and depositing her jeep with the most competent mechanic she could find, Cynthia took a bus to the city of Puebla to visit Mexican archaeologist Juan Armenta Camacho. Although he was not professionally trained, Camacho was a serious amateur who was searching through fossil beds in hopes of discovering manmade tools. Infected with his enthusiasm, Cynthia offered to return and help him after her own research was completed.

In the meantime, through the help of a friend in Mexico City, Cynthia had located a site near the town of Tulancingo, Hildalgo, where she began her most important excavation of the year. About this time, however, Braulio had to return to other duties so she continued her explorations by herself.

Many of the places she visited, she now admits, were once "where a young single female should not go alone." The Huastec Indians of San Luis Potosi, for instance, had the reputation of being uncivilized and dangerous. Some people said that they had "never seen five pesos at one time" and were ready to "kill you for your boots." Although these local rumors were no doubt exaggerated, it is true that poverty had made the Indians desperate.

When the wealthy rancheros in the area met Cynthia and learned what she was doing, they unsuccessfully tried to dissuade her. They then offered to make things easier for her by providing laborers, burros, and tools. "One of them," she recalls, "decided I shouldn't be running around by myself without any armanent, so he gave me a very nice chrome-plated .32 revolver. Well, of course I don't use guns, but at that time I could certainly use the money. So I hocked the gun to buy supplies and gasoline."

Despite help from the rancheros, Cynthia found herself in serious financial shape as the winter wore on. Her purchase and repair payments for the jeep took such huge chunks of her NSF income that she was forced to supplement her grant by moonlighting at another job. In Tulancingo, near the site she was excavating, she therefore went to work as a kitchen helper in an old-fashioned inn to earn room and board and a little money to buy gasoline for

Cynthia Irwin-Williams *Photo by Barbara Williams*

her jeep. Eventually she was promoted to being a cook in the inn's restaurant, and now brags that she is a "pretty good Mexican cook."

On one occasion Cynthia decided to explore the mountains near the town of Ixmiquilpan, a mission that required the services of a guide. She appealed to the town fathers to locate someone for her, and they obliged by offering to release a convicted murderer, named Geronimo Gomez, from the local jail. Although he had been incarcerated for getting in a bar fight with a fellow Otomi Indian and fatally stabbing him, the town officials considered Gomez harmless. They assured Cynthia that they let the prisoner out of jail frequently to do various tasks, such as sweep the courthouse steps, deliver newspapers, or cut lawns. The officials told Cynthia that further proof of Gomez's docility was that he had spent all his time in jail knitting sweaters. Customers would bring him yarn and pay him to make the sweaters. "He probably had more money when he was in jail than he'd ever seen before," Cynthia speculates.

Once before in Mexico Cynthia had taken a chance and gone off to the backcountry with an Indian she hardly knew. Braulio Garcia had proved to be trustworthy enough, but Cynthia knew she would be taking a far greater risk to put herself in the hands of Geronimo Gomez, a known murderer. Nevertheless, she either had to let him serve as her guide or risk the far more likely possibility of getting lost in the mountains. She therefore decided to accept the word of the town officials about Gomez's character.

One day, with the convict beside her in the jeep, Cynthia was exploring the hills when suddenly the heavens broke. The ensuing rainstorm washed out the arroyos, and she was trapped for two days with a sentenced murderer and no food. Fortunately her guide proved to be as gentle and considerate as the authorities had vouched, and she returned to town a few days later hungry and tired but perfectly safe.

All in all Cynthia's experiences on her first archaeological trip to Mexico were fascinating and useful, and Lady Fortune protected her in circumstances where, as a young woman, she was quite vulnerable. Successful as her experiences were, however, she wouldn't recommend to other woman that they try to follow her example.

On that first trip Cynthia developed some important friendships and made good contacts for subsequent excavations in Mexico. In 1962 she returned to that country to begin her first major independent research project in the archaeology of early man, a subject which at that time was surrounded by mysteries and controversies. Her excavation at Valsequillo in the Mexican state of Puebla, proved the existence of manmade artifacts in situ with a wide range of Pleistocene fauna: extinct species of horses, camels, mastodons, mammoths, sloths, tapirs, and giant tortoises. The carbon 14 dating of remains at one site indicated an age of 21,850 years, which was much earlier than many archaeologists had previously believed that Stone Age man had existed in the New World.

Lasting four years, the Valsequillo project was conducted with the help of several other people, including coinvestigator Juan

Armenta Camacho, who had interested her in the excavations initially. Her mother, who had accompanied Cynthia to Mexico, was also of enormous help to Cynthia. When the Mexican authorities refused to allow American archaeologists to remove artifacts from the country, Mrs. Irwin developed techniques for making plaster and plastic reproductions of the important objects. Eventually she gained an international reputation for her specimens. Her reproductions are now on display in museums in Europe and Canada, as well as in the United States, and her techniques have been adopted by museums all over the world.

The excavations at Valsequillo were conducted mainly in the spring. During the winter months of 1962-64, Cynthia graduated from Harvard with her Ph.D., married David Williams, spent a year as a postdoctoral fellow at the American Museum of Natural History, and began her teaching career at Eastern New Mexico University. Initially she was hired only half-time at twenty-four hundred dollars a year, but she eventually became a full-time professor, recognized for her distinguished classroom performance as well as for the archaeological digs she conducted with student volunteers.

Some of her projects and papers were researched in collaboration with her brother, Dr. Henry T. J. Irwin, who was an associate professor of archaeology at Washington State University at the time of his premature death in 1978. The best known of their middle-1960s' excavations, the important paleo-Indian site of Hell Gap, Wyoming, was the work not only of Henry and Cynthia but of their close friend George Agogino.

As a result of her own unhappy experience as a student volunteer on her first archaeological dig in Europe, Dr. Irwin-Williams has formulated her own philosophy about the manner in which field crews should be treated. "I've always tried to have a good balance of men and women," she says, "partly because it's socially much more pleasant and partly because it's more fair." However, the applicants are accepted on the basis of their individual references and not on any kind of fifty-fifty quota. Dr. Irwin-Williams also accepted people of various racial, ethnic, religious, and linguistic backgrounds long before the civil rights movement gained momentum, and she has also taken people with a variety of handicaps, including amputation, total hearing impairment, and cerebral palsy. "Everyone deserves a chance," she firmly maintains.

No doubt because of Irwin-Williams's obvious sense of fair play, her integrated crews are noted for their camaraderie. One of the few violent incidents that has ever taken place during a field trip was provoked because members of her crew were protecting each other. During an excavation at Hell Gap, a bar fight erupted in the nearby town of Guernsey when a customer insulted a black member of her crew. Immediately his fellow workers turned on the slanderer, starting a general brawl which was quieted down only after Dr. Irwin-Williams was called to the scene.

Day-to-day living on Irwin-Williams's field trips is made more pleasant by a minimum number of rules and the rotation of camp duties. She also encourages games and parties but doesn't supervise them too closely, preferring to treat her student volunteers as adults rather than as children at a summer recreational camp. She considers herself a professional archaeologist, not a house mother nor a social director.

Dr. Irwin-Williams, right, inspects trowel work of a student *Photo by Barbara Williams*

Dr. Irwin-Williams, center, conducts author Barbara Williams, left, around excavation at Salmon Ruins, New Mexico

The largest, the most spectacular, and undoubtedly the most important excavation of her career so far has been the one she began in 1970 at Salmon Ruin in northern New Mexico, two miles west of Bloomfield on Highway 64. Named for George Salmon, who homesteaded in the area in the late nineteenth century and protected the site from vandals, Salmon is a huge Chaco Indian pueblo, shaped like a squared *c* and measuring 400 feet along the back wall, 150 feet along the sides, and extending two stories high. The Chaco people, whom Dr. Irwin-Williams discusses with considerable respect, built this huge "apartment" of 250 rooms between 1088 and 1095 A.D., using engineering principles comparable to those employed in Europe at that time.

Probably the most sophisticated of the various pueblo peoples, the Chacoans built miles and miles of perfectly engineered roads, designed elaborate irrigation systems, and developed complex as-

Cynthia Irwin-Williams examines data to be fed into the computer *Photo by Barbara Williams*

tronomical interpretations. They lived in an agricultural society, growing corn, beans, and squash, which they supplemented with game.

The modern inhabitants of San Juan County, where Salmon Ruin is located, have known about the Chaco dwelling for more than a hundred years, but they have lacked the funds and skills to excavate it properly. In about 1969, led by local enthusiasts Alton James and Harry Hadlock, they approached Irwin-Williams for help because of her reptuation for dealing successfully with volunteers. "Since I started out in an amateur society myself," she explains, "I have every sympathy for them, and not all archaeologists do."

With funds contributed by the National Endowment for the Humanities, the National Science Foundation, the state of New Mexico, the Four Corners Regional Commission, the National

Cynthia Irwin-Williams, left, confers with an assistant *Photo by Barbara Williams*

Historic Sites Preservation Commission, the Navaho tribe, and San Juan County itself, Irwin-Williams undertook the various phases of the work at once. The formal excavations began in the summer of 1972 with a staff of 120 professionals and volunteers. In each of the next six summers, the digging resumed, with many of the same crew members coming back every summer.

Besides studying the apartment itself and uncovering small artifacts, the archaeological team hoped to learn about the forces that motivated the Chaco society. What kind of organization did the Indians have that enabled them to achieve such remarkable engineering feats? What was the relation between the social and the religious elements of their lives? What caused the demise of their society in the middle of the twelfth century? What happened to the people?

Answers to many of these questions will be provided in the published reports of the Salmon Ruin project, a many-volume series that is barely underway. However, Irwin-Williams sees more far-reaching benefits from the excavations than simply the addition to our knowledge about a single group of pre-Columbian Indians. For one thing, the project contributed to a healthy community spirit. For another, it helped train many volunteers who went on to become professional archaeologists.

For the first few years of the Salmon Ruin project Irwin-Williams obtained some crew members by advertising in the newsletter of the Society for American Archaeology; but as word spread about the magnificent training that she was making available, she was inundated by applications. Former volunteers were sending her two or three times as many friends and relatives as she could use, so she had to stop advertising for workers.

The Salmon Ruin project has also contributed to Irwin-Williams's personal growth. "Because of its size," she explains, "it has enabled my research team and me to explore new methods and techniques which would not have been possible in a smaller program."

As the Salmon Ruin project winds down, there are many other things to fill Irwin-Williams's time. Her university contract specifies that she spend three-fourths of her academic year doing research and one-fourth of her time teaching. Altogether, she devotes up to seventy or eighty hours a week in some activity related to archaeology, including the meetings and paperwork required by her positions.

Admittedly, she is a workaholic, and the commitment to her career (which was fostered long ago by her mother) has sometimes put a strain on her marriage. Her husband had difficulty, especially during their first years together making the compromises that were expected of him. He saw the need for her to follow her professional career but had hoped her schedule would be closer to a normal nine-to-five workday. It took him several years to accept their rather unorthodox lifestyle and her overattention to her job. Thus Dr. Irwin-Williams advises young women to think twice before following the course she did: "I would say if there's any way of avoiding long-term commutes, married couples should try to do so. They are difficult and disruptive and require a very high level of commitment on the part of both husband and wife."

Dr. Irwin-Williams and an associate at Salmon Ruins consider a difficult problem
Photo by Barbara Williams

In addition, Irwin-Williams thinks an archaeological career poses problems even for unmarried women. "In the beginning I found it very difficult to combine the two contradictory roles of being a woman and being an aggressive and ambitious professional archaeologist. It was particularly hard to maintain a normal social relationship when I was the employer or 'boss' of the men in the group."

Despite these problems, Irwin-Williams cannot imagine herself in any other career but that of archaeologist. "Archaeology offers all of the usual benefits of a highly interesting academic career. In addition, because of its very special character, it offers some of the excitement of the chase and some of the mystery-solving delights of an Agatha Christie novel. Finally, it offers the same kind of reward that any kind of scientific experimentation or exploration offers its afficionados."

One of Cynthia Irwin-Williams's employees summed up all these arguments more succinctly: "This work is the most fun a person can possibly have and still get paid for it."

Jane Kelley at Tula, Hidalgo, about 1953 *Photo by Arturo Romano*

CHAPTER 2

JANE HOLDEN KELLEY

AMONG WOMEN ARCHAEOLOGISTS Jane Holden Kelley is almost one of a kind. In fact, her colleagues are frequently awed by the way she balances her professional career with her other roles of wife and of mother of a large family. Many women have found archaeology and domesticity to be incompatible and have reluctantly given up one or the other, but Dr. Kelley has proved that being a good archaeologist doesn't necessarily mean being a bad wife and mother—or vice versa.

Several factors probably account for Dr. Kelley's success. For one thing, she was a mature woman (just two months short of her thirtieth birthday) when she married, and by that time she had finally resolved the long and painful identity crisis she experienced as a girl. At the time of her marriage she not only had learned to understand herself and her priorities, but she had also learned to like herself, too.

For another thing, Dr. Kelley actually enjoys many aspects of domestic life. She's an excellent cook, who takes pride in whipping up interesting meals for her family and their friends; and she has never resented the time her four children have required of her even though she gave birth to twins while she was still writing her doctoral dissertation in her late thirties.

For a third thing, her husband, David H. Kelley, is also an archaeologist and therefore understands how much of her energy his wife must spend preparing to teach and advise students at the University of Calgary (in Alberta, Canada) and in doing her private research. "Dave doesn't mind a messy house," she explains.

"Indeed, he opposes my cleaning binges because I get exceedingly bad-tempered, stomping around, raving about how lazy everyone else is. As it is, we run a household that isn't hazardous to the health of the inmates, but it's a far cry from the housekeeping Dave's mother did."

Jane's father, W[illiam] C[urry] Holden (himself a college professor), summarizes the situation by claiming that Jane keeps the different aspects of her life in separate compartments. "I think that is right," she agrees. "People who only meet me at meetings often don't realize I have four children, or any children. People who know Dave and me somewhat superficially sometimes marvel that we maintain such a stable marriage since we are so different. People who know us well wonder less often."

For a husband-wife team of archaeologists teaching at the same university, David and Jane Kelley have many differences. Dave much prefers library research to field work, specializing in the preColumbian Indians of Mesoamerica. "He hates working in interrupted bits and pieces," Jane explains, "and to really get into serious work on calendars or glyphs or whatever, he needs blocks of time when he is rested and can submerge himself totally without interruptions." Jane, on the other hand, turns her "thinking" time on and off with greater ease, adjusting naturally to the immediate demands of her household.

Additional personality differences are reflected in the kinds of meetings they attend. One would expect a husband and wife engaged in the same career to attend professional meetings together. Not the Kelleys. Jane likes the big meetings, like those held by the Society for American Archaeology or the American Anthropological Association, but she is seldom successful in coaxing Dave to accompany her. Even when they do travel together, they split up at the conference and operate independently.

The Kelleys have been married more than twenty years (since June 11, 1958), but David Kelley wasn't the first anthropologist in his wife's life. Although her mother, Olive Price Holden, died when Jane (born Narcissa Jane Holden in Abilene, Texas, on August 31, 1928) was only nine years old, Mrs. Holden's avid interest in the cultures of the various Indian tribes was to have a profound and lasting influence on Jane and on Jane's father. Trained as a librarian, she took several anthropology classes as an undergraduate student at the University of Texas in the 1920s and

Left to right, standing: Don Pablo Martinez del Rio, Marie Wormington, Jane Holden Kelley, Manuel Maldonado-Koerdell, Carlos Margain, and, kneeling, Luis Aveleyra de Anda *Photo by Arturo Romano*

subsequently focused particular attention on the anthropology and archaeology sections of the libraries where she worked. Jane Kelley recalls that her mother spent considerable time copying sections of Henry Rowe Schoolcraft's two-volume *Algic Researches* and loved to pore over the English translations of Navaho chants.

Probably the most tangible evidence of her mother's interest in anthropology was the house in which Jane spent her girlhood. Soon after the family moved to Lubbock, Texas, where Dr. Holden taught at Texas Technological College and Mrs. Holden worked as a librarian, Olive Holden decided she wanted a house that would be in keeping with the landscape. She therefore designed an adobe structure patterned on pueblo architecture and persuaded her husband to build it himself. As Jane points out, "That house and the two adjacent adobe houses my father built later are now more or less considered cultural heritage landmarks, but they were regarded as rather eccentric in Lubbock of the 1930s when Indians and Indian crafts were not so socially acceptable in west Texas as they have since become." Eccentric or not, the Holdens completed the first adobe house and proceeded to furnish it with handmade chairs and tables, Navaho rugs, and paintings by southwestern artists. It was the home of Mrs. Holden's dreams, and for several years it was the only kind of house that her daughter, Jane, knew.

In addition to the influence she exerted on her family's physical surroundings, Mrs. Holden played an important role in her husband's subsequent teaching career. With no formal anthropological training, he was hired to teach only history classes at Texas Tech, but because of his wife's strong attachment to the Indians of the Southwest, Dr. Holden moved into anthropology through the "back door." Soon after they settled in Lubbock, Dr. Holden began undertaking archaeological field work in west Texas and eastern New Mexico, though ironically enough, his wife seldom went with him. (She was a "Victorian lady," Jane recalls, who hated the living conditions in archaeological camps and preferred to learn about Indians from books.) Then, in time, Dr. Holden encouraged the college administration to let him introduce beginning anthropology courses into the history department curriculum. Eventually the anthropology classes became more varied, but for the next twenty years they were still offered only through the history department and Dr. Holden was the only professor to teach them.

Students registered for Dr. Holden's anthropology courses apparently because the classes were enjoyable—not because they might lead to a serious career. "If any of the students from the early 1930s went on to become full-time anthropologists," Jane Kelley reflects, "I am not aware of who they might be. Rather, innumerable students from that era in later years made a point of telling my father that although they became farmers or bankers or engineers or school teachers, they found to their great surprise that the anthropology courses he offered were the best 'training for life' they received in college."

However, adults of that era were highly agitated over the kinds of information that students were gleaning from Dr. Holden's anthropology lectures. This was only a few years after John T. Scopes had been convicted in Tennessee for teaching Darwin's theory of evolution in the public schools, and religious fundamentalists in west Texas were just as anxious to make sure that their college-age sons and daughters were not exposed to "sinful" Darwinism, which conflicted with the story of the Creation in the Bible. On one occasion Dr. Holden put his own job in jeopardy by supporting a fellow history teacher who had been denounced from pulpits all over Lubbock for advocating social reforms and for suggesting that a scholarly approach to the Bible would make it possible to reconcile modern science with certain Old Testament stories.

As the schism grew between intellectuals on the Texas Tech campus and angry churchmen who preached that drought and other local problems were God's punishment of a wicked community, where among other things some people denied the Bible was literally true, Dr. Holden became the direct target of inflammatory sermons. Jane Kelley still recalls a "fundamentalist minister standing on a street corner across from the college handing out tracts denouncing evolutionary exhibits in the museum, naming my father as the perpetrator of the heresy."

Thus, in the atmosphere in which Jane spent her first few years, West Texans didn't always share the Holden family's commitment to knowledge and understanding. Whereas Mrs. Holden had raised eyebrows in Lubbock for choosing to live in a house that looked like an Indian pueblo, Dr. Holden—though he was warmly admired by students—aroused anger in some circles for the things he taught at the college.

Jane, however, took little notice. She was mainly aware of the facts that her family lived in an "Indian looking" adobe house and that in the summer Dr. Holden went on field trips to uncover real Indian artifacts. "My father's brand of anthropology was partially characterized by depression-style ideas about how to do a lot of digging on almost no money and by the mystique that anthropology was exciting and wonderful, but no way to make a living. Texas Tech was somewhat isolated from other centers of anthropology and from other anthropologists, and it was not sending many students out to become professional anthropologists. But it was by no means completely isolated, and the caliber of the courses and the field work was quite respectable for that period."

Although her mother seldom stayed overnight at the excavations, Jane was frequently toted along. She started accompanying her parents at such an early age she can't even remember her first archaeological dig. Her father still teases her by repeating a story from her early childhood. Among some mastodon remains his field crew uncovered a projectile point—an item that was so significant (because it proved that humans had existed in North America at a much earlier time than had previously been believed) that he took it home for safekeeping. But Jane promptly lost it. Dr. Holden now jokingly suggests that Jane became an archaeologist in order to make amends for losing that very valuable artifact.

Her father tells that story so frequently that Dr. Kelley is certain it must be true, but she has very cloudy recollections of such early episodes in her life. Clearer memories date to the period later in the 1930s when her father alternated summer expeditions to Arrowhead Ruin near Santa Fe, New Mexico, and to Mexico City. "My role seems to have been that of obnoxious child," she admits, in describing those summer excursions. "Sometimes students let me dig or screen, and sometimes I imitated adult behavior by keeping my own field notebook, in which I carefully recorded the details of cutting up worms." She was particularly gleeful when she could record her finding of a shard or arrowhead in the backdirt that the students had already excavated and screened. Such a coup, of course, proved that their recovery techniques were not 100% accurate and that she was a better archaeologist! "All of these experiences," Kelley reflects, "were as ordinary as visiting my grandparents' farm. In truth, I wasn't interested in archaeology—it was just there. I don't suppose I learned any cultural history at all, except that those ruins were 'old.'"

In 1937 Mrs. Holden died, and Jane's secure and familiar world evaporated. While Dr. Holden adjusted to his own personal loss and eventual remarriage, Jane was shunted from a Catholic boarding school to her grandmother's house and from her grandmother's house back to the boarding school, with brief intervals on a ranch with her aunt. All of these moves only intensified Jane's anxiety and increased her difficulty in making friends. When she finally returned home during her high school years to live with her father and new stepmother, she was out of step with them and with the other teenagers in Lubbock. As she currently observes, "With the wisdom of hindsight, I have to say that I was somewhat emotionally disturbed. A more miserable misfit would have been hard to find."

Today Dr. Kelley admits she was lucky to have both a mother and a stepmother who "placed a high priority on intellectual, political, and community activities." At the time, however, she could see only the differences between the two women. Her mother was a refined, old-fashioned "lady" who read a great deal and ran the household with live-in students as substitute servants. "By the time Fran [Jane's stepmother] came along," she says, "that life-style was less feasible, but I was there to help with housework during my high school years while Fran taught geography to pre-flight students during World War II." A much more vigorous woman than Jane's mother, Frances Holden kept an immaculate house and served fantastic meals. She also went on every dig with her husband, pitching in as necessary to cook for the students or to assist with the excavating. So willing to work herself, Frances Holden set high standards for Jane, demanding that she too do her share of the cooking and cleaning.

Jane's problems in adjusting to a stepmother were complicated by the fact that she was an outcast at school. As she then perceived the other girls in her Lubbock high school, they were dating constantly and making plans to get married as soon as they graduated. They certainly had no inclination to chum around with an insecure transfer student who had no boy friends. Jane now concludes that her lack of popularity with schoolmates of both sexes was as important as her parents' interest in anthropology in leading her toward a professional career. "If I had been a social success in high school," she speculates, "I would undoubtedly have married by age eighteen. As it was, I did weird things like taking arc welding as part of a plot to run away to the California ship yards if my life became less bearable. Like my mother had done before me, I 'lived' through the books I perpetually read, none of which were remotely related to anthropology."

Alienated at school and unsure of herself at home, Jane found refuge in the college anthropology museum where she did odd jobs for her father to earn spending money. The familiar old museum was the only real link she had with her past, and Jane retreated to it after high school classes and on Saturdays to spend her time "washing museum cases and removing mammoth femurs from their plaster-of-Paris jackets."

World War II was winding to a close when Jane graduated from high school in 1945, and in a sudden spurt of self-reliance she found a job as a clerk-typist at a nearby air base. Joining a car pool and earning a regular salary made her feel grown-up and independent, especially since the job also provided access to the officers' club, where she could listen to war stories exchanged by the men who had recently returned from the European theater. For the first time in years she felt worthwhile and reasonably happy. But her father had other plans for her. College. Reluctantly she resigned from her civil service job in the fall to register as a freshman at Texas Tech. As she relates, "I dutifully enrolled as a premed major for no better reason than I had no direction and my father thought it would be nice to have an M.D. in the family because they *did* make a good living."

The career choice was disastrous. Not really interested in medicine, Jane failed to give the introductory courses her best effort, and though she managed to stay afloat during her first year, she submerged under the difficult science curriculum in her second. As a sophomore she failed qualitative analysis and barely passed comparative anatomy with a D and physics with a D−, the latter grade bestowed only on condition that she exit at once from the premed program. Thus she became a history major, with excursions into animal husbandry, astronomy, and other unrelated subjects.

Conversely, once she entered college, Jane's social life revived as unexpectedly as her academic life foundered. Invited to join the prestigious social organization called the Ko Shari Club, Jane convinced herself that she was extended a bid on her own merits and not because her parents were faculty sponsors nor because her mother had helped found the club in the early 1930s. Jane read Willa Cather's *Death Comes for the Archbishop*, required of every pledge, and over the Easter recess traveled with the other girls to a restored kiva at Arrowhead Ruin, where she participated in an initiation ceremony that her mother had paraphrased from Navaho chants.

Outwardly Jane was a minor social success, but inwardly she alternated between trying to establish an identity completely apart from her family and enjoying the advantages of being the daughter of an important faculty member. By that time William Curry Holden was head of the history department, dean of the graduate school, and director of the museum. Although her home was within walking distance of the college, Jane chose to live in the campus dorm, deliberately avoiding Dr. and Mrs. Holden for long periods at a stretch. Furthermore, her fierce desire for acceptance by friends her own age led her to participate in so many all-night dorm sessions that during her freshman year she became ill.

Following her nose dive in the premed program and against everyone's advice, Jane registered for her father's course in introductory anthropology and discovered, much to her amazement, that she was genuinely interested in a subject in which she also did well. New ambivalence developed as she wrestled with her desire to major in anthropology and her fear that fellow students would believe she was getting preferential treatment from her father if she did.

"For his part," Jane relates, "my father was equally ambivalent—pleased at my interest but afraid I would be led away from the training that would eventually net me a good job; he still did not regard anthropology as a reasonable career choice. We struck a bargain that I would take anthropology, but the balance would be a minor in clothing and textiles in the home economics department. (My aunt, just then, had a good job as a home economist with the Rockefeller Foundation in Peru.)"

Jane completed her junior year at Texas Tech as an anthropology major. The following summer, in 1948, the college resumed its archaeological field schools, which had been suspended since the beginning of the war. Jane received college credit by participating at Arrowhead Ruin under the supervision of Dr. William Pearce. Today Dr. Kelley regards that first field experience as low-key and the other students as a "mixed bag." They included teachers who needed a summer course to renew teaching credentials, a Baptist preacher who spent most of his time leaning on his shovel and quoting the Bible, and a few people genuinely interested in archaeology.

Her graduation from Texas Tech in the spring of 1949 was rewarded with a wonderful present from her parents—a summer trip to Mexico City to live with archaeologist Eduardo Noguera, who served as head of pre-Spanish monuments, and his wife Mona. This double-pronged learning experience provided the chance for Jane not only to learn Spanish but to accompany don Eduardo to the archaeological sites he routinely visited. As an added bonus, Jane joined the class of American college students that Bill Pearce brought down to Mexico in July. In short, she "fell madly in love with Mexico and one or two Mexicans."

When fall came and she had to return to the United States, she still had no goal before her, so she followed the line of least resistance and entered the University of Texas at Austin to begin study for an M.A. degree in anthropology. The summer in Mexico had intensified her interest in anthropology and archaeology, but, like her father, she wasn't absolutely certain if archaeology was a viable career choice or just a pleasant "life enrichment" program.

Graduate school in Austin proved to be one of the happiest periods of her life, both academically and socially. With its broader anthropology faculty, the University of Texas exposed her to a variety of completely new philosophies—real "mainstream stuff." Furthermore, she found the city a delightful place in which to live, and she began to form lifelong friendships with anthropology students and professors. Although most of the teachers knew her father, she at last felt she was succeeding on her own. Almost.

In the summer of 1950 she returned to Lubbock for the first of seven seasons with the Texas Tech field school at various sites in southeastern New Mexico, where she functioned in the ill-defined roles of student, field boss, and cook. Despite the fact that her first summer's excavation at the Bonnell site provided the basis for her master's thesis (she received her M.A. from the University of Texas in 1951), she worried now and then about the quality of training in the Texas Tech summer programs. "I wanted to go to Point of Pines for some first-rate training," she recalls, "but somehow I always went to New Mexico. Those field schools were long on enthusiasm and digging and short on resources, at least when compared to today's standards. An incredible amount of energy went into the business of living—digging latrines, putting up tents, hauling water, cooking, washing dishes." In retrospect, however, she realizes that her seven summers in New Mexico were invaluable, not only for the training they provided in field methods but for the interesting material she collected.

One difficulty at the time was that the Texas Tech programs seemed to attract students who were more interested in camping experiences than in archaeology, and Jane remembers how the young crew members would shirk their duties to try to capture the various forms of wildlife: lizards, rattlesnakes, tarantulas, and vinegarroons (huge scorpions that emit a vinegarlike odor when they are startled).

For her own part, Jane tried to keep as much distance as possible between herself and wild animals—particularly the skunks that invaded their camps periodically. She recalls one summer when the skunks enjoyed such a population explosion that they were causing problems for the entire area, getting caught in hay bailers and provoking the neighboring ranchers to carry loaded guns. Jane herself became paranoid about the animals, which were ejecting foul odors throughout the countryside. She began lacing her tent tightly each evening to keep the skunks outside, a strategy that one night proved counterproductive when a skunk found its way into the blackened tent and was unable to find its way out again. Jane lay rigid throughout the interminable visit, waiting for the worst to happen; but fortunately the uninvited guest finally escaped without serious consequences.

Another episode took place during a heavy rainstorm when the Ruidose River, where they were camped, overflowed and washed away the archaeologists' outhouse. The flood occurred at a time when many visitors, including Dr. and Mrs. Holden and Dr. Holden's "gorgeous blond secretary," were in the camp. Dr. Kelley recalls how the campers grabbed the objects dearest to them and tried to carry them to safety. One woman rescued her cosmetics. Another drove her new car to high ground. Some overweight archaeologists hurried to the kitchen to save the food. A diarrhea victim anxiously seized her bottle of medicine. But Jane snatched all the valuable artifacts she could carry. Almost without realizing it, she had declared herself an archaeologist.

Unlike other women who have become archaeologists, Jane's entrance into the profession was easy—if anything, too easy—because of her father's position. At the earliest stages of her career she was actively involved in more or less running field projects and was accepted as an archaeologist by the other archaeologists she met. No one ever told her that archaeology was a man's world, and a great many men actively encouraged her. Perhaps because her life was so enjoyable and access to archaeology was so easy, she had not yet made long-range career plans.

When she heard about the E. D. Farmer Scholarship to Mexico, she decided to apply. This is a grant offered through the University of Texas that carries the unusual stipulation that applicants must be Texans of Texas-born parents. A fifth-generation

Texan on her mother's side and a second-generation Texan on her father's, Jane was eminently qualified on those grounds, but somewhat to her surprise she met the other requirements as well and was awarded a renewable fellowship (for two years, as it turned out) to study at the Escuela de Antropologia in Mexico City. The Escuela proved to be very different from the American institutions she had attended, with late afternoon and evening classes taught by busy anthropologists and archaeologists, most of whom held down several other jobs. The curriculum provided considerable opportunities for travel, and she learned a great deal about Mexican sites.

Jane lived in Mexico throughout most of 1952 and 1953, during which time Luis Aveleyra and other archaeologists excavated the San Isabel Ixtapan mammoth in the northern part of the valley of Mexico. So noteworthy was this particular find (manmade tools were found among the mammoth remains, giving evidence of a very early hunting society in that part of the world) that several people specializing in the archaeology of early man, including E. H. Sellards, Alex Krieger, and Marie Wormington, were invited to observe the discovery. Up to that time Jane had not seriously considered getting a Ph.D. in anthropology and was still working through the conflicting attitudes she had absorbed in west Texas. On the one hand were her early high school notions about popularity and appropriate roles for women and on the other was the reality of having already moved away from these youthful perceptions.

In these circumstances, Dr. Wormington's appearance in Mexico made a significant impression on the younger woman. As Dr. Kelley now explains, "Whatever the deep and dark intricacies inside my head, Marie Wormington was the right role model at the right time. Everyone involved in the San Isabel Ixtapan find seemed to comment on what a gracious lady she was, and having previously shared a cabin with her at an archaeology conference, I already knew she read mystery stories. Somehow the combination of a smart, respected professional woman who was human enough to read mysteries seemed an unbeatable combination. And I suppose I had worked my way far enough through my own numerous hangups to be able to start making decisions. My moment of truth didn't come immediately. It struck some weeks later about 3 A.M.

Weddıng party, Lima, Peru, June 1958. Left to right, Norah Andrade, Jane Kelley, David Kelley, Dwight Wallace, and, in background, Gabriel Lasker

one dark night as I was riding on a bus between Jalapa and Mexico City."

Once the decision was made, Jane began to consider which graduate school to attend. After visiting its campus, she rejected the idea of studying at the University of California at Berkeley, because a graduate student told her that archaeology students there got embroiled in a faculty feud; she dismissed UCLA on the grounds that Los Angeles was too urban for her tastes; she wavered between universities in Arizona (because of her interest in the Southwest) and Seattle (because a professor in Mexico had recommended it). But Fred Wendorf, whom she had known in New Mexico, told her firmly that she should go to Harvard. Never expecting the Harvard admissions committee to look beyond the C's and D's on her sophomore transcript, she mailed off her application for entrance and was stunned when she was accepted. "I think they were spreading the geographical representation of their students at the time," she explains.

Emboldened by this unexpected vote of confidence from Harvard's graduate school, she set off for Cambridge, Massachusetts, in the fall of 1954. "My newly stiffened resolve wilted a bit when I attended my first class, a seminar on Peruvian archaeology under Gordon Willey," she recalls. "The other eight or ten students seemed fluently verbal; also they appeared to know so much about the subject I wondered why they were there. I left the class feeling out of my league, and I seriously considered closing my unpacked suitcases and catching the train home." The problem was not merely that the others knew more about Peruvian archaeology than she did because she figured that with extra effort she could catch up on that. What really troubled her was that the other students expressed themselves so eloquently and had such broad backgrounds in art history, economic theory, sociological theory, philosophy of science, geology, and Greek literature.

Psychiatry was her particular stumbling block. To her, Freud was merely the founder of psychoanalysis, whereas the other students "discussed what he meant in a footnote and what the Freudian revisionists made of this or that point." "Indeed," she says, "I never did catch up, and I deeply regret to this day my superficial knowledge of so many subjects that do have real and important implications for anthropology. The only compensation is that I have found I am not alone, which doesn't make it better, only less lonesome."

Jane was in residence at Harvard for three years. Considering herself lucky to be admitted to Harvard at all despite her appalling undergraduate record, she didn't apply for the few highly competitive fellowships available. Instead, she helped to support herself by serving as a teaching assistant in a large introductory class, acting as a Radcliffe housemother, and typing papers for other students.

During that period she encountered another graduate student in archaeology, David Kelley, but is embarrassed to report that neither one of them can remember their first meeting. Their paths crossed on campus as well as at social functions, but they didn't really start to date until 1957. In the spring of that year David graduated and left for Peru on a Fulbright research fellowship, and Jane completed her residency at Harvard and returned to Texas.

While attending Harvard, Jane had returned to New Mexico each summer to continue her assignment as field director for the Texas Technological College summer field sessions in archaeology. At the time she had no intention of using those experiences for a Ph.D. dissertation but had arranged with the Mexican government to do her doctoral research at the site of Tula, Hidalgo. As things worked out, however, she was fortunate to have spent seven summers compiling notes in New Mexico.

Winding up her classwork at Harvard in the spring of 1957, Jane received word that her father was seriously ill and that she was needed in Lubbock to take over his classes at Texas Tech. Before leaving Cambridge, she attempted the first major hurdle toward her Ph.D., the oral examination. This was held in the informal smoking room of the Peabody Museum, where, under the interrogations of several faculty members, she gave "a less than sterling performance" but nevertheless passed.

Once back home in Texas she divided her energy the next year between teaching anthropology classes at Texas Tech and writing intense letters to a Fulbright scholar in Peru. As soon as school was over in June 1958, she flew to Lima, where she became Mrs. David Kelley in a wedding ceremony witnessed by most of the American anthropologists working in Peru. After a very informal "reception" at the Pension Morris, she and David worked for two months and then toured South America before returning to Lubbock.

Although by that time Dr. Holden was well enough to resume teaching, David Kelley was hired as an additional member of the Texas Tech faculty (at less than three thousand dollars a year) and Jane served as a research archaeologist for the museum (without pay). They both assumed that Jane would proceed with reasonable haste toward the completion of her Ph.D., which meant she would have to abandon her plans to do new doctoral research at Tula, Hidalgo, and to substitute data she had already gathered during her seven summers in New Mexico. What they hadn't anticipated was how much time Jane's family responsibilities would consume after the arrival of her first child, just nine months after her marriage.

Although Dave and Jane were delighted about the arrival of Rebecca Ann (Becky) Kelley in March, Becky's birth sorely taxed their finances (the obstetrician's bill was five-hundred dollars, or

Jane Holden Kelley, Sue Willard, Bill Glover, 1953 at Penasco Valley, New Mexico *Photo by Earl Green*

one-sixth of their total income that year), as well as their careers. Jane Kelley now admits that if she had known in 1959 how difficult it would be to complete her Ph.D. while raising a family, she never would have attempted it; but by taking her problems one day at a time she somehow managed to fulfill all of her responsibilities.

"The first year or two were the worst," she recalls. "We were poor. Every month ended in beans. I didn't have a graceful first pregnancy, and Becky had colic for weeks. My postpartum recovery was slow, probably because of the drugs I was given for the delivery." Having never been around babies, Jane was a nervous mother who at first didn't even feel comfortable holding her daughter; and the situation wasn't helped at all by an authoritarian pediatrician who discouraged breast feeding and insisted Jane give Becky solid food before the baby could tolerate it. Luckily, Jane switched to a warm and sensitive female doctor, under whose care both the mother and baby became happier and more relaxed.

That period was a difficult one for David Kelley, too. Totally inexperienced as a teacher, he was suddenly confronted with five courses each semester for which to prepare classes and to deliver lectures. He also made the mistake of assigning more term papers than he had the time to read. Averaging three or four hours of sleep each weeknight, he survived that first year only by sleeping until noon on Sundays.

In time they worked out arrangements that allowed the household to function while Dave wrote and taught and Jane completed the primary analysis of the three tons of New Mexico artifacts she had gathered during summer field schools. Both of the Kelleys worked with the South Plains Archaeological Society, and Jane found time to return to half-time teaching. She also collaborated with Earl Green (a paleontologist at the museum in Lubbock) on a study of previous archaeological work that had been conducted at Lubbock Lake, an important site of early man near Lubbock.

In 1963, with four-year-old Becky and two-year-old Thomas Michael, the Kelleys said goodbye to Texas and went to Uruguay for six months. Dave had once again received a Fulbright fellowship, this one giving him the opportunity to serve on the Faculty of Humanities in Montevideo. Upon completion of that assignment, the Kelleys settled in Lincoln, Nebraska, where David began

Dr. Kelley as associate curator of anthropology, Nebraska State Museum

teaching at the University of Nebraska at a substantial increase in pay.

Jane's three tons of artifacts were left behind in Texas. Now she faced the business of turning the voluminous notes from her earlier analysis into a dissertation. The dissertation, however, proceeded in fits and starts, partly because she had become associate curator of anthropology at the Nebraska State Museum, and partly because she gave birth to twins—a boy, Dennis Walter Curry Kelley, and a girl, Nancy Megan Kelley—in 1965.

The next year, when Jane had just about used up all the time that Harvard would allow her for writing the dissertation, she girded up for a herculean push. This required huge quantities of cooperation from family, colleagues, and even babysitters. On one occasion she hired a babysitter named Marcia to watch her children while she worked on her thesis. Apparently more neighborhood children converged on the premises than Marcia could oversee, and one of them built a fire on Jane's coffee table. "Marcia sent one of the children up to my thesis hideaway to tell me," Jane recalls. "I replied, 'Tell Marcia to put it out,' which I must say still seems to me to have been reasonable." Marcia, however, thought Jane was a bit too detached under the circumstances, but she wrote up the episode for an A in her English class.

Jane's dissertation was accepted by her Harvard committee, and she was finally awarded the Ph.D. degree—nine years and four babies after she had completed her course work. However, she realized that although she had at last acquired her credentials, she had been left in the dust of her contemporaries from Harvard days, all of whom were five to ten years ahead of her in professional achievement.

Jane Kelley also suspects that her struggle to finish her dissertation while caring for so many small children may have slowed down her husband's career too because she relied on him for so much help. She recalls one morning in Nebraska when a former student was staying at their house. "I offhandedly asked Dave to take out the garbage," she relates. "The student was stunned—finally gasping, 'Now I understand why he doesn't publish more.' It takes years for Dave and me to work through our major research to publication. His glyph book was in progress for umpteen years."

No sooner had she submitted the final version of her dissertation and drawn her first easy breath than her father approached her with a new writing project. For years Dr. Holden and his wife had been compiling the autobiographical data written by a Yaqui (Mexican Indian) named Rosalio Moises for a future book, but Dr. Holden was too busy with other research to shape the material into the format that his publisher wanted. Since Jane's dissertation had finally been completed, her father asked if she wouldn't like to undertake the project, and she readily accepted.

Her job was to edit the notes Rosalio had set down in broken English so that his sentences would be comprehensible and his chronology and family names consistent. Inasmuch as Rosalio could barely speak English, Jane spent long hours talking to him in Spanish, making copious notes, and eventually producing *The Tall Candle*, a biography that is not only highly readable but rich in anthropological insights.

During the time Jane was working on Rosalio's book, a friend telephoned from Canada to ask if both Dr. Kelleys would be interested in flying to Calgary to be interviewed for two positions in the archaeology department at the university. Because the salaries

At the autographing of *The Tall Candle* at the Texas Tech Museum. Left to right, Jane Holden Kelley, Ana Valencia, Thomas Michael Kelley, Francis Holden, Curry Holden

were considerably better than the ones they were earning in Nebraska, they were very interested indeed, and the following year they began their joint careers in Canada.

Teaching for the first time in ten years was very difficult for Jane Kelley. In addition to the problems that David had encountered at Texas Tech when he first started teaching, Jane discovered that the discipline of archaeology had changed while she had been caring for her children and writing her "eternal" dissertation. "I was sadly out of date," she admits, "and updating was added to lecture preparation. In some ways I was nearer despair at this time than ever before. It was worse than my initial reaction to Harvard erudition because this was a road I thought I had covered, only to find I virtually had to start over, beginning with a new vocabulary." When she tried to read the professional journals she couldn't even understand them because so many new techniques and philosophies had surfaced since she had been in graduate school. It required nearly two years of concentrated effort before she felt comfortable about what she was doing.

Once Jane caught up again with contemporary archaeology, her professional life began to mature. She enjoys teaching, especially the ongoing contact with a new generation of graduate students, and frequently visits them to supervise field work they are conducting at archaeological sites. In the summer of 1969, for instance, such supervisory trips took her from British Columbia to Ontario and from the Arctic Ocean to the United States border of Canada. She was also enormously pleased to be elected treasurer of the Society for American Archaeology and to serve on that organization's executive board. Jane notes with wry humor that after she was named to the position, she was told that she had been chosen because she represented two different minority groups—women and residents of Canada.

Ironically, Jane discovered that her interrupted career provided certain advantages because she had virtually a clean slate for beginning new research. With funds from the Social Sciences and Humanities Research Council of Canada (sometimes called the SSHRCC or Canada Council), she began a study of the lives of Yaqui women. This very flexible and personalized form of research was compatible with her other responsibilities, and after several years of research and writing, her book *Yaqui Women* was published in 1978. Her Yaqui research also provided her with the data for short professional articles.

Returning to archaeological field work was slower than ethnological research because Jane felt she couldn't cope with both family responsibilities and the organizational demands of such projects. However, in 1975 she undertook a modest field project in southeastern New Mexico. Later that same year she accompanied Dr. Peter Shinnie, a colleague at the University of Calgary, to the Sudan for a month's stay at Meroe, a large archaeological site in the Nile Valley.

One of the ways in which Jane was able to carry out research without assuming the organizational commitments of a field project was to restudy the three tons of artifacts she had used for her doctoral dissertation years before. For that study she had employed the "comparative approach" (the standard archaeological method in the 1950s), while sitting in an old barn and classifying potsherds by color and type as birds flew over her head. As the years passed, Jane felt that her huge collection of artifacts deserved more sophisticated and specialized analysis than had been possible earlier. She therefore obtained a grant from the Canada Council to have her materials shipped to Calgary so she could subject them to scientific techniques that had been adopted by archaeologists in the years since she had completed her dissertation.

As Jane explains, "This is the sort of thing that will happen more and more in the future. In years to come archaeologists will have fewer opportunities to excavate because they are simply running out of sites where they can dig. That means that archaeologists of the future will spend their time subjecting materials already excavated to new methods of scientific analysis. My project was significant because it was a trial case in seeing how much more information can be learned from materials that have already been carefully studied once."

In the summer of 1979 (when her twins were a grown-up fourteen years of age), Jane embarked on a substantial archaeological excavation. Karen Bruhns (see chapter 3), who had worked at Cihuatan for several summers, invited Jane to participate in a field study at what may be the largest site in El Salvador. Since in graduate school Jane had considered Mesoamerican archaeology her specialty, the invitation offered her a chance to return to her first professional love. In addition to working on this project, Jane is currently coauthoring a book with Marsha Hamen on scientific methodology in archaeology.

Jane Kelley's career to this point in her life follows a pattern fairly common for professional women: adolescent identity crisis, encouragement from professionals, interruption and resumption of career, and the process of catching up. Fortunately, the profession of archaeology provides enough flexibility so that all these potential difficulties have worked out rather well for Jane. Both Kelleys consider themselves extremely fortunate: David and Jane are full professors at the same university; they are happily established in Calgary and have had a hand in training perhaps one-fourth of all the professional archaeologists in Canada; that country has been good to them; and they have not had to face the agonizing decisions of married couples who can find only one suitable job for the two of them or who must take jobs far apart.

Although Jane admires those married couples who collaborate in their work, collaboration is not a part of the Kelleys' style. Jane explains it this way: "The secret of our marital survival is complete noncompetition. This means, for me, remaining fairly remote from Dave's primary interest because we think so differently that conflict would undoubtedly emerge if we tried to cooperate. I do not attempt to understand at any deep level the glyphs, calendars, genealogy, trans-Pacific contacts, or other subjects near and dear to his heart. Dave couldn't care less about Yaquis and he doesn't particularly like the Southwest, which I adore."

Such detachment allows them to appreciate each other. Jane relates with considerable astonishment and pride how Dave participated in a group of four archaeologists who were working to decipher some Mayan glyphs. "They portrayed, in a microcosm, something very like an interdisciplinary approach. Each controlled different sorts of information and had different perceptions. They yelled at each other, tested, challenged, beat on whatever was handy. The cooperation was as complete as I have ever witnessed, and the end product probably shaves twenty years off the evaluation and testing procedures that would have been necessary shakedown time if they had all done their thing in isolation, slowly reacting to each other in print."

Jane Holden Kelley has been able to combine marriage, four children, and an archaeological career. For her, anthropology and archaeology are a way of life. Both Kelleys feel very fortunate to be able to do what they love best and get paid for it. They find the puzzle-solving aspects of archaeology endlessly intriguing. Being archaeologists has allowed them to see many parts of the world they might not have visited otherwise. Making modest contributions to the understanding of the human condition, past and present, has been intellectually and emotionally satisfying. But best of all, they feel archaeology is fun.

Jane Kelley and Robert Clement-Jones sorting ceramics in the Sudan, 1975 *Photo by Sam Gerszonowicz*

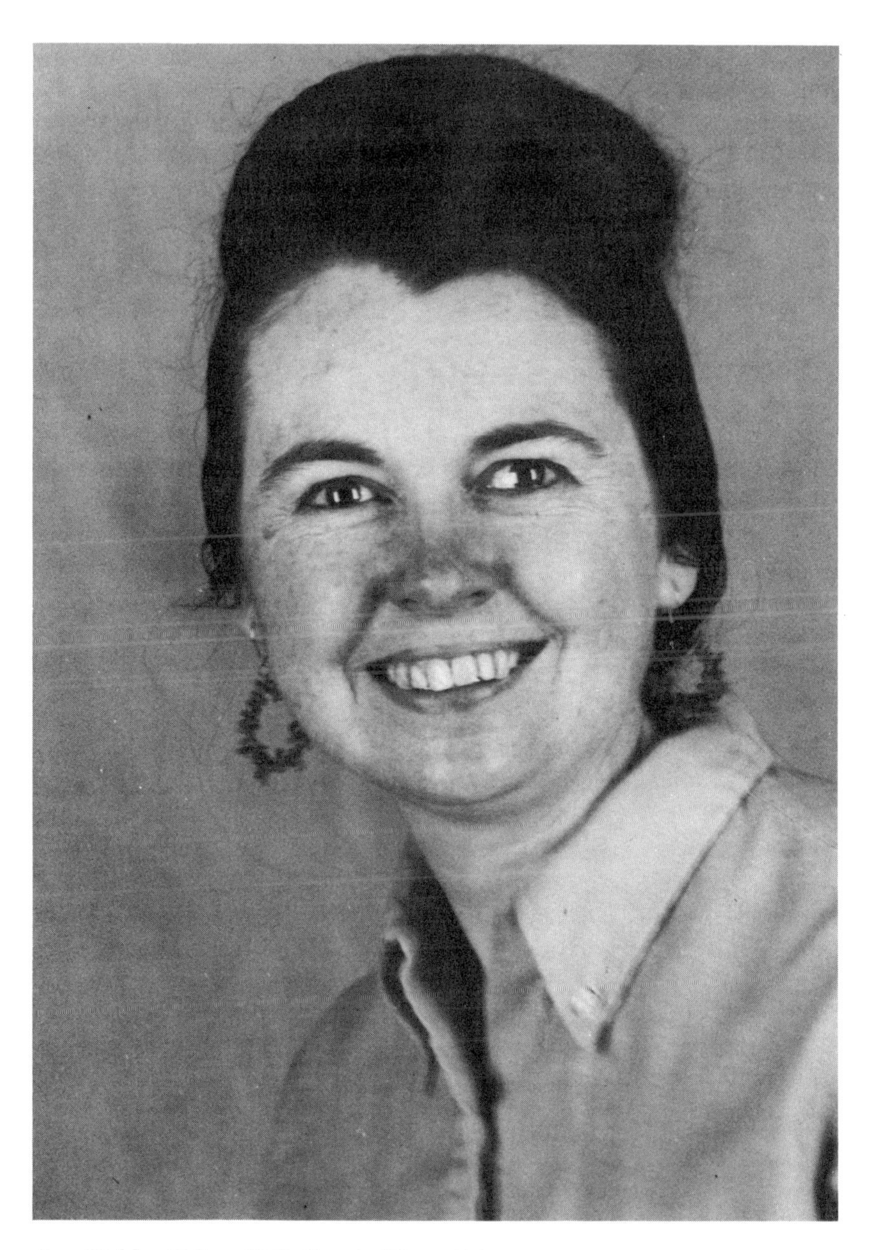

Jane Holden Kelley, 1967 *Photo by Wayne Nelson*

Karen Bruhns, surrounded by handmade pillows, relaxes in her back-yard hammock *Photo by Barbara Williams*

CHAPTER 3

KAREN OLSEN BRUHNS

"ARCHAEOLOGISTS HAVE TO FIGHT their way to the top," Karen Olsen Bruhns often warns her students at San Francisco State University. "Ladies especially shouldn't go into this profession unless they're tough."

If "tough ladies" seems like a contradiction in terms, many other things about Dr. Bruhns are enigmatic, too. A small, fragile-looking woman, she dresses conservatively, in outfits that have a quaint Charleston-era charm—lavender print sheers, for instance—and moderately high heels ("My feminist friends tease me about the way I dress," she explains. "What they don't understand is that when I go into the field I spend weeks and months sweating in the same grubby clothes. When I come home, I like to dress up.")

Dr. Bruhns's modest duplex in Berkeley, California, shows considerable evidence that it is occupied by someone with a traditional interest in the homemaking arts—a carefully nurtured rose garden, a small patio with a hammock, and many hand-embroidered pillows strewn about. She shares this comfortable home with a man named Thomas Weller, a graphic designer, a partner in a small publishing firm, and the most significant person in her life for the past eleven years. Dr. Bruhns, who was married briefly in the 1960s, has old-fashioned ideas about commitment but is taking her time about tying the knot a second time. ("My friends amuse themselves by planning my wedding and one of these days Tom and I shall do it . . . no hurry at this point," she explains.)

Altogether, Karen Bruhns throws strangers a bit off balance because she looks like one kind of woman and talks like another. The truth is that Dr. Bruhns has many facets, any one of which can flash unpredictably at a given moment.

If you visit her at her home in Berkeley, she may conduct you through the bedroom to a small study, apparently added to the duplex as an afterthought. The study is clearly a work area, its walls lined with makeshift shelves filled with books, manuscripts, and cartons of film. Two expensive-looking cameras rest on tripods.

In that private sanctum, where she is accustomed to working alone, Dr. Bruhns appears edgy with a stranger present. She fiddles with an ashtray and doesn't quite know how to begin the conversation. She offers you a drink, and when you refuse, she pours herself a glass of bottled mineral water. ("California tap water isn't always potable," she says. "You should see our hepatitis rates. I got hepatitis here in California—not South America—but I got into the habit of drinking mineral water because too much coffee gives me coffee nerves and soda pop is fattening.")

Feeling the need to put her at ease, you comment on her attractive smile. "My teeth are crooked," she demurs, calling attention to one front tooth that protrudes just a little and paradoxically makes her smile more interesting. "My family couldn't afford orthodonture when I was growing up. Some of my friends think I should get braces now. But I don't think it's worth it. I'm afraid of pain."

Within just a few minutes you have seen many of the conflicting elements of Karen Bruhns's personality. The college professor who talks to students interested in archaeology about the necessity of "fighting" has turned out to be a diminutive, feminine woman who likes to embroider, fusses over her roses, is nervous around strangers, drinks bottled mineral water, and avoids pain. Then without warning, Dr. Bruhns lights a cigarette, puts her dainty feet on her desk, and begins to talk.

"I'll tell you about archaeologists," she volunteers. "We're all prima donnas. All the successful ones. There is a definite personality selection for being aggressive, particularly if you're a woman. The ladies who make it through graduate school are the ones who have learned how to tell other people where to get off. By that time the instinct to kill has to be pretty well developed."

In Karen Bruhns's case, the gladiatorial skills were honed long before college days. As a child she had to assert herself or be tyrannized by the two males in her family, a father with a violent temper ("Pop and I both yelled a lot," she admits) and an older brother who was chronically ill and accustomed to being waited on. Thus her apprenticeship for "aggressive lady archaeologist" began in her preteen years when she learned the importance of "standing tough."

This doesn't mean that Karen Bruhns was necessarily born tough, however. As a matter of fact, she came into this world prematurely, on April 19, 1941, a scrawny little thing who was not expected to survive. During her infancy and preschool years she was so tiny and frail that her parents, William and Verna Olsen, hovered over Karen almost as much as they did over their son, William, born a few years earlier with a heart defect.

Then suddenly—about the time of Karen's fourth birthday and the time the senior William Olsen moved his family from Santa Rosa to Placerville, California, in hopes of finding a better job in his trade of garage mechanic—Karen started growing. Soon she was taller and huskier than all her friends, an unkempt tomboy ("My braids were always coming undone," she relates) who ran off her excess energy playing baseball with the neighborhood gang or staying after school to play basketball. These games with her friends also gave her an excuse to stay away from home, where she often felt she was trapped into waiting upon her invalid brother, who languished in bed, and into doing his share of the household chores.

By the age of ten she had reached her full adult height of 5 feet 3½ inches—a physical superiority that lasted only until her sophomore year in high school, when the other kids once again started looking down onto the top of her head. A few painful accidents on the basketball court with burlier players convinced her that she wasn't cut out to be an athlete, and she started spending more time reading. "We had a lot of books at home," she recalls, "and I literally read everything I could get my hands on. Our local county library was small and didn't have best-sellers and the like, but it had a whole lot of very good books, including old travel and archaeology books. I read the original *Tomb of Tutankhamen* when I was a sophomore, along with Leonard Woolley and Kathleen Kenyon books. Then I found out about interlibrary loan and started getting books from all over."

In school, however, she was bored much of the time. Her social circle did not value the acquisition of good grades (nor were her girl friends particularly interested in dating), and not all of the teachers in her rural high school were wise enough to keep the brilliant teenager motivated. Her senior year was a particular waste. She had completed all the requirements for college entrance by the end of her junior year, but the school administration insisted that she keep her seat warm for another year. As a result, her classroom performance was erratic, though she did get A's in the subjects that held her interest—English, Spanish, and history—and she qualified for honors when she entered college.

Years earlier she had become addicted to reading *National Geographic Magazine* in her school library and was particularly fascinated by issues reporting on archaeological excavations in Egypt. She had always known she wanted to go to college and learn more about history and ancient cultures. Furthermore, she was fairly certain that she could obtain a scholarship to study at one of the University of California branches.

Persuading her parents to permit her to go to college was the real challenge. Although both of them had gone to college briefly (her mother had attended a junior college for two terms, and her father had studied at Stanford University until the depression forced him to go to work), they saw no need for university training, especially for women. More importantly, they had no money to help Karen in school, and her father worried that she would end up as he had—quitting school because of money problems and spending the rest of her life as a frustrated college dropout. Both parents firmly believed she would be much happier if she accepted the conventional role for Placerville girls, graduating from high school and then working in the local bank or dime store until she got married.

Knowing how her parents would react to her plans, Karen delayed telling them until the last possible moment that she had applied for admission to the University of California at Berkeley and had passed the entrance exam with a high enough score to receive a four-year state scholarship (awarded to students in the upper 10 percent). She also had received an additional scholarship of four hundred dollars, which would help pay for her room and board her first year away from home.

"Pop and I had a large shouting match when the two scholarships came in," Bruhns recalls. By then, however, Placerville, California, was at the height of the pear-canning season, and Karen was working almost around the clock at the local fruit-packing plant. That meant she had a legitimate reason for ducking out when the fighting got too shrill. Verna Olsen didn't react quite as angrily as her husband, but she was very disappointed in her daughter and felt that Karen was somehow letting down the family. Mrs. Olsen became reconciled to archaeology as an appropriate lifestyle for someone in her family only many years later, after Karen had earned her Ph.D., had found a steady job, and was "obviously having a good time while remaining solvent."

Tempers flared so hotly in September 1959, however, it seemed that Mr. and Mrs. Olsen would never accept the idea that their daughter wanted to go to college. But despite the yelling, Karen proved she had the mettle to become a "tough lady archaeologist" and held fast to her decision to go to the university. As soon as the pears were sorted and canned, she grimly began packing her belongings. Almost as grimly, Mr. and Mrs. Olsen agreed to drive her to Berkeley, but by the time the threesome had reached the university campus, they were all a bit misty-eyed.

At Berkeley, new kinds of problems surfaced for Karen, including the basic one of having to provide food and shelter for herself. Unable to type well enough to find "ladylike" employment in an office, and realizing that babysitting didn't pay too well, she accepted whatever domestic work she could find—scrubbing floors, washing windows, and polishing furniture. Between working so hard and enjoying the stimulating social life ("For the first time in my life I discovered there were actually interesting men," she recalls), she seldom had the inclination to study, and her first semester's grades "weren't really swell." By her second semester, however, she was able to schedule her time better. Her grades went up, and she was able to maintain them high enough to get her scholarship renewed.

Another problem was the need to convince the male-dominated faculty and student body of the Berkeley anthropology department of her determination to become an archaeologist. As she relates, "I got a lot of crap from male professors and a certain amount from my peer group since I wanted to get out and dig, not marry an archaeologist."

Fortunately for Karen, one member of the faculty was highly supportive of her efforts. During her freshman year, she met Professor John H. Rowe at an anthropology department party, where she gratefully discovered that he was not only very courteous to beginning students but also "was one of the few people who didn't say, 'But you will just get married and have babies, dear.'" Aware of the problems that women students faced in dealing with other professors, Rowe "took his students on ability and didn't discriminate in any way, shape, or form on the basis of sex."

Rowe particularly admired Karen because she was studying the classics—something he thought more archaeology students should do. In time, he hired her as a reader for his lecture course in comparative civilization and after she reached graduate school he provided her with an opportunity to serve as his research assistant. With his keen ability to size up students after his first meeting with them, he assumed from the beginning that, woman or not, Karen had the spunkiness to get through graduate school and the good sense to get her life together and go out into the field.

In addition to Rowe, another member of the anthropology department provided Karen with encouragement though of a slightly different sort. "At that time," Karen explains, "Dr. May Diaz was one of the few female faculty members, so she served as a role model for all the women students. She was living proof that you could have a family, a career, and still be a woman. We all watched her interaction with her colleagues very carefully." Equally interesting was her feminine appearance, a clear refutation of the myth that female archaeologists were lumpy creatures who waddled around in hiking boots and oversized sweaters. "Dr. Diaz," Bruhn readily notes, "happens to be a stunning woman with fabulous taste in clothes."

Rowe and Diaz were the exceptions, unfortunately. The anthropology profession was then undergoing a period of transition, and women were just beginning to do field research on their own. Many male archaeologists simply did not take their female colleagues seriously, expecting them to stay within the more traditional specialties, such as linguistics, ethnology, and museum work. This attitude led them to restrict the opportunities with which they provided their female students ("We haven't the facilities for two toilets, dear," was an excuse Karen heard frequently), and women could not get the excavation experience necessary for their professional growth. Field assignments were often limited to opportunities on the local digs, within daily commuting distances of college campuses. And even on local excavations the women were assigned the dullest tasks, such as working the screens.

Other male archaeologists seriously believed they were doing female students a favor by pointing out the difficulties of trying to combine a career calling for field work with marriage and child rearing. Thus John Graham (who has since changed his philosophy and now takes women into the field on a regular basis) sincerely tried to persuade Karen to become an epigrapher, a specialty within anthropology one could master while working genteelly at home or in a library. Graham thought Karen would adapt readily to the subject because she had a strong background in foreign languages and could draw extremely well. What he neglected to note was that she was "bored to death by sitting around trying to figure out ancient texts."

However, Karen could not have accepted any opportunities to participate in exotic, far-away summer archaeological excavations, even if she had been offered them. Throughout her college years, she set aside her summers as periods to work full time and to save extra money for her study-filled winter months. With little financial support from her family, she was not in a position to pay her fare to an excavation somewhere in Europe or Latin America, particularly if she were expected to serve there as a volunteer.

Therefore, her first assignment on an important field trip did not occur until after she had graduated, and even then she received the offer only indirectly. By June 1963, when she obtained her B.A. degree, she had been married about a year to Dan Bruhns, who was still an undergraduate student in anthropology. Someone thought he would make a good archaeologist and offered him a job with a mapping project in central Mexico, allowing Karen the privilege of tagging along.

For many reasons that first field trip, which should have been an exciting experience for the brand-new anthropology graduate, was a genuine dud. Karen soon discovered that even those rare females who did make it into the "field" inevitably wound up in a laboratory: Although she had wangled her way onto an archaeological crew in a foreign country, she was not allowed to work outdoors with the men but was assigned to a lab with several other indignant women. "After a lot of yelling," Bruhns recalls, "we got the great boon of one day a week outdoors picking up shards, which wasn't even digging. The reasons given were sunstroke and a lot of other stuff that struck me as so dumb that I didn't bother to remember it. It is easy to be flippant about it now, but at the time we were all livid."

An even more serious problem stemmed from the fact that not merely the project director but all the other males, including Karen's husband, had stereotyped attitudes about sex roles. It infuriated Karen that after a hot day, when both of them had been working for ten hours and wanted to sit down and relax, Dan expected her to play the role of "nurturing woman," taking care of his needs and bringing him "nice cups of coffee." As a result, they quarreled a great deal, as did most of the other people on the crew.

With strong letters of recommendation from John Rowe and John Graham, Karen returned to Berkeley in the fall to begin work on her Ph.D. in archaeology. Her undergraduate grades hadn't demonstrated her full potential as a scholar because she had frittered away her first semester and had spent so much energy trying to support herself. Nevertheless, her grade point average was respectable (she graduated cum laude), though not high enough to qualify her for one of the two teaching assistantships in archaeology, which seemed to be awarded to male students anyway.

Although Karen was later allowed to serve as a teaching assistant for one summer term, for the most part she supported herself in other ways. Her language skills, for instance, opened special doors, and as she explains, "I got a lot of reader and research assistant jobs because I could read French and Spanish and muddle my way through Portugese and Italian—skills my fellow students didn't have." On the whole, however, she "fought" her way through graduate school. "I spent a lot of time scrubbing floors and cleaning ovens to pay the rent, but I got straight A's as a grad student except for the no-credit course in German. John Rowe lined all of us, male and female, up against a wall and taught us German, at least enough to pass the exam." During her last semester as a graduate student, when she was writing her dissertation, she held down two cleaning jobs, one research assistantship, a readership, and a job at the Fillmore Auditorium.

The dissertation itself posed problems because she wanted to do its research in Colombia but didn't have the money to go there. Getting funds for her research was very difficult because most graduate students do their dissertation field work as part of a bigger project. Among her professors only John Rowe realized that her desire to conduct field investigations in Colombia was resourceful. Rowe, she explains, "hassled the administration until

Karen Bruhns in 1966 on her first field trip to South America, working on her Ph.D

they came up with some funds, but only enough for three months in the field."

Meanwhile her marriage, which had started off on the wrong foot, was stumbling badly. She and her husband had irreconcilable personality differences, but for the sake of her parents (who were deeply religious and were still scandalized over a divorce that had taken place in the family thirty-five years previously), she hung on. As Karen worked singlemindedly toward her goal of professional archaeologist, Dan tested a variety of careers, including archaeology, art, and filmmaking. Finally, in 1966, when Karen left him at home while she went off to Colombia to do the research for her dissertation, she realized how terrible her marriage really was. Instead of being lonesome for her husband, she was enormously pleased not to have him around. On her flight back to the States three months later, she worried about how to tell him she wanted a divorce, but she arrived home to find that he had run off with someone else. A great relief.

Back on the Berkeley campus, things looked cheerful, too. The professors who had registered misgivings about her dissertation research in Colombia were impressed by what she had accomplished there. "I came back with tons of material," she recalls. After thinking about the dissertation for six months she wrote it in six weeks, hiring a typist with a small grant she had received for that purpose.

Karen completed the dissertation in time to receive her Ph.D. in the spring of 1967, a year when antidiscrimination laws were being implemented and universities were suddenly seeking out women for teaching positions. Within anthropology departments, faculty positions were first made available to women in ethnology, a specialty that Dr. Bruhns explains "was heavily funded by the feds." However, the new attitude "slowly began to slop over into archaeology, too."

As this new climate of equal opportunity for women was settling over the nation, John Rowe received a long-distance telephone call from a friend at the University of California at Los Angeles, asking if he knew of a qualified holder of a Ph.D. who would be willing to accept a one-year appointment to UCLA's anthropology faculty. Rowe gave Bruhns an enthusiastic endorsement, and she moved to southern California for one academic year.

When that year was up, Dr. Bruhns located another teaching job at the University of Calgary in Canada. "I went to Canada initially," she recalls, "because they offered me good money, and I needed a job." In hope that the position would be a permanent one, Bruhns gave it her best effort. She threw herself enthusiastically into preparing for lectures, and in the summer obtained money from the Social Sciences and Humanities Research Council of Canada (SSHRC) for field work in South America. In 1969 she worked in the Andes with one research assistant. The following summer she returned to central Colombia for an archaeological site survey with a staff of four people.

Bruhns was hired to go to Calgary the same year that Jane Holden Kelley (see chapter 2) and her husband David joined the archaeology faculty there. The three newcomers became fast friends, but the Kelleys enjoyed Canada more than Bruhns did. It didn't take Karen too long to decide that Canada was too cold for her—literally and figuratively—and she resigned after two years.

In retrospect Bruhns feels that archaeology's professional status is not significantly different in Canada than it is in the United States. What had upset her was that the women's movement had not caught fire in Canada, and after struggling so hard to achieve her freedom, she was reluctant to return to what she regarded as "provincial values." In 1968 women in Canada were "definitely second-class citizens," she asserts. "I couldn't cope with people calling me 'dear' and 'little lady' and things like that. At parties all the women went to one corner and all the men to another. If you went and talked with your male colleagues instead of sitting with the women to discuss floor wax and the servant problem, you got lots of horrible looks."

Actually, it was the Canadian weather that finally got to her. As she explains, "I decided that I couldn't stand Calgary any longer when I looked out of my window one day. There was a blizzard outside, and the temperature was fifty-five below. I thought if God had arranged for me to be born in California, he probably hadn't intended for me to spend my adult life freezing to death in arctic conditions." Bruhns was therefore delighted to find a new job in northern California—at San Jose State University.

She had already received a grant from the Canada Council for field research, so the summer before she moved to San Jose she

Dr. Bruhns and two students from Calgary in 1970, washing off petroglyphs in Rio Espejo, central Colombia. This was the first scientific archaeological study of the Quimbaya that did not rely on looted artifacts

went to central Colombia to conduct a site survey and excavation. Inasmuch as no archaeology had been conducted there previously, she attracted considerable interest. Some people were nervous about all strangers because it was a time of violence in the country, with numerous kidnappings, murders, and other savage crimes. Some people were merely curious as to what archaeology was all about and what Bruhns was doing in their country. She was interviewed by reporters, and through the media her face became known to a number of Colombians.

Since many of the natives were treasure hunters and tomb looters, archaeologist Bruhns was naturally identified with them. In fact, some of the wealthiest and most widely known families in Colombia had acquired their fortunes through generations of robbing graves, so perhaps it is not too surprising that even the rob-

Karen Bruhns excavating a tomb in central Colombia, 1970

bers themselves assumed that she was one of them. One such person, who operated a wealthy coffee plantation by day and robbed graves by night, took Bruhns into his confidence. He told her about, among other things, the bodyguard he kept to protect him against the people who were always after him—kidnappers, because of his enormous wealth, and lawmen, because of his nefarious nighttime activities. He also told her about another tomb looting he was planning on his coffee plantation (it is illegal in every country of the world to rob ancient sites for personal profit, even if such sites are on one's personal property) and invited her to join him.

Bruhns weighed the alternatives carefully. As a professional archaeologist, she certainly didn't believe in tomb looting and didn't want to be a party to it. On the other hand, she knew she could never prevent the plantation owner from digging on his own property. If she went along peacefully, she could at least take notes that might be of benefit to science.

Reluctantly Bruhns agreed to meet the looter at the specified time and place. At the last minute, however, she discovered that the bodyguard was unable to come along and that she was supposed to serve as "lookout." When the robber handed her his pearl-handled .45 and told her to guard him, she protested that she didn't like guns and had never used one. But he was insistent. He instructed her that if anyone approached them, she should close her eyes and shoot, holding the gun high enough so that she wouldn't hit her own feet.

Bruhns didn't have to use the gun that night, but the grave robber wasn't the only person in Colombia who thought that a lady should be able to handle weapons. When she went to a store to buy a machete for clearing land to begin her archaeological survey, everyone assumed she was buying it to "protect her honor." She denied she had any need to protect herself in such a violent way, so a couple of her friends concluded that she was much too innocent for her own good. They insisted on giving her careful instructions in how a lady uses a machete in moments of crisis.

Despite all such lessons in weaponry, Bruhns asserts that her life was never in peril on that trip to Colombia. The only times she has ever been afraid about her safety during archaeological field trips in Latin countries were when she was riding a bus. Latin bus drivers, she claims, have little compunction about getting drunk while on duty—particularly after dark. Sometimes the passengers, too, are liable to become intoxicated and surly.

Returning to the States in the fall of 1970, Bruhns began teaching at San Jose. Among the courses assigned to her was the undergraduate class in field work—a course designed to provide students with the basic skills and techniques used in archaeological excavations. This meant that she had to operate some digs near the San Jose campus, within commuting distance of the school. California archaeology is not especially to her liking, but for two years she operated two digs in northern California, one in conjunction with a professor from the University of California at Santa Cruz, for the benefit of students.

The field work course was normally limited to about twenty students. On Saturdays and Sundays the students kicked in for gasoline to drive to the particular excavation, and on Wednesday nights they examined their findings in the college laboratory.

"When I ran my first field class," Bruhns recollects, "I decided to do something about sex stereotyping and laid down the law that the women got equal time on the shovels and trowels. I got a lot of hassling from the women about that. They broke their fingernails and ripped their clothes because most of the girls had no idea about the way to dress for physical labor."

Bruhns no longer teaches field classes in California, but when she takes students on excavations out of the country, she schedules some briefing sessions first, discussing such things as how to dress, how to handle a pick, and how to get into physical condition before doing tough outdoor work.

Since moving to the faculty at San Francisco State University in 1972, Bruhns has been successful in arranging many archaeological field trips in Latin America. "I've had fewer problems with paper work and with getting permission for digging than a lot of my colleagues have had," she says. "I lay this to the fact that John Rowe very carefully trained us in the diplomatic procedures of working in another country." Furthermore, women archaeologists from North America don't pose the threat to Latins that male archaeologists do. "Local people don't realize that a woman can be engaged in archaeology as a serious lifetime profession and assume it is simply a temporary job before marriage," she explains.

Getting money to dig is another problem entirely. American institutions that grant funds for archaeological research do not have confidence in women as project supervisors. "The people up here," Bruhns complains, "think that women will not be able to interact properly with the natives or that women will be sick all the time. They just don't consider us professional equals to the men."

In addition to conducting her own research in Latin countries, Bruhns has visited other people's excavations. During the summer of 1973 she "bounced" around South America, stopping for several weeks in Peru with John Rowe and his wife at an Incan site near Cuzco. "They asked me to stay," she explains, "and I became the general dog Spotty, shopping and cooking and running the errands that people usually do when they visit a dig."

On the whole, that field experience was a happy one because the Rowes established good social relations with the local Peruvian archaeological establishment through consultations, parties, and

Karen Bruhns on a cold morning in 1973 in Tiahuanaco, Bolivia

numerous visits. Bruhns recalls, "We all spoke Spanish on the excavation all the time so that any passerby wouldn't think we were trying to hide anything. That's something John Rowe always insists upon."

By contrast, her next field experience the following summer was disastrous—the worst one of her life. She was still recuperating from a serious bout with hepatitis in 1974 when the curator from the San Francisco State Museum and a Nicaraguan archaeologist persuaded her to conduct a site survey on Zapatera Island in the middle of Lake Nicaragua. The Nicaraguan intended to serve as the director of the excavation and said he had made all the preliminary arrangements, such as obtaining a survey permit, renting living quarters, and arranging for food and equipment. Thus Bruhns, who was still a bit shaky after her illness, would have few administrative responsibilities about which to worry.

The first clue that details for the field trip weren't well organized emerged at 10 A.M. on the day that the crew was supposed to leave the shore of Lake Nicaragua for the island. The ten-foot motor launch was waiting at the dock, as scheduled, and the crew members were ready to leave. But the director had not yet gathered and packed the necessary provisions. It took until 4 P.M.—six hours after the planned departure—to get all the equipment onto the tiny craft.

By then the sky was black with ominous clouds. Bruhns begged the director to postpone departure until the next day after the storm had passed, but he insisted on leaving immediately. No sooner were they beyond the reach of shore than a violent storm erupted. Furthermore, the director had not bothered to ascertain exactly where the island was located, and the boat tossed about in frightening waves until midnight.

Finally, they reached the island and raced to the porch of their rented house, only to discover that the director had neglected to bring the keys. Unable to get inside, the crew members huddled on the porch until the storm subsided the next day and someone could return to land for the keys. Meanwhile, they had nothing to eat but the coconuts lying about.

From that dreadful beginning, events grew even worse. The director began digging holes in mounds, although he admitted he had no digging permit. After challenging him about this unprofes-

Dr. Bruhns, right, and a student, beginning the excavation of a patio floor in Cihuatan, El Salvador, 1977

sional behavior, Bruhns discovered he had openly lied to her about something else. He hadn't even acquired the survey permit he claimed he had. Irately she arranged for the motor launch to return her to Granada and announced to the other members of the crew they could join her or not, as they wished. The archaeological site has since been destroyed, and Bruhns's few field notes from her survey are the only data that remain.

It is not surprising that Bruhns is now very edgy about codirecting archaeological digs with anyone she does not know well. Even then she likes to understand in advance exactly what the lines of authority will be. In 1975 she began a project in El Salvador, working at first with a small mapping crew. Securing additional funds, she returned the next three years with student crews to excavate what turned out to be an important site in the

Mesoamerican trade network of about 900 A.D. In 1978, however, the crew foreman who had accompanied her each previous year was unable to leave the United States, so Bruhns assumed the foreman's job as well as her own position as director.

In the midst of that hectic summer of 1978, Bruhns was corresponding with her friend Jane Holden Kelley in Calgary, complaining about the problems she was having in trying to do two jobs. The two women agreed that it would be pleasant to go to El Salvador together in 1979 and codirect the project. Kelley had been unable to do any field work for many years because of family responsibilities, but now her children were old enough to leave at home. Thus Bruhns and Kelley decided to apply separately for funds to take students from their respective schools to El Salvador in 1979 to continue the research.

Ironically, Kelley received the full grant she requested in Canada (see chapter 2), whereas Bruhns was unable to obtain any funds. This meant that Kelley would have a large crew of students to supervise, and Bruhns would have to take a secondary role in the project she had started. With no hard feelings for her close friend, Bruhns backed out. She went to El Salvador in 1979 only long enough to introduce Kelley to the local people and to show Kelley what she [Bruhns] had already accomplished with the excavation.

Failing to obtain funds for one summer did not put a serious crimp in Bruhns's archaeological plans for the future. She conducted field work in Belize in January 1980 and has in mind for the next few years several other projects for which she has good prospects for obtaining funds.

Young people eager to go on an overseas field project with Bruhns or another archaeologist may be interested to know how she selects her crew members. "I like women on my staff," she admits frankly, "because you can usually count on them to be responsible for themselves." She finds she has the most problems with married men—particularly those over the age of twenty-five—because they have developed the habit of letting their wives wait on them. Bruhns expects her crew members to tie up their own hammocks and mend their own clothes. She doesn't have the time or energy to be "sweet and motherly." She is a professional archaeologist, not a nurse or servant.

Karen Bruhns in her home office in Berkeley, August 1979 *Photo by Barbara Williams*

Dr. Bruhns has further advice for high school girls who are thinking about archaeology as a future career. "Learn some math," she emphasizes. "Math is incredibly necessary these days, and it isn't stressed enough for women." She believes that the failure of grammar school and high school teachers to impress on girls the importance of learning math has been a significant reason why women have been kept out of many careers. She also urges young people to study drafting, foreign languages, and automobile mechanics—all of which are useful at one time or another on an archaeological field trip.

Most archaeologists won't take high school volunteers on excavations until they are sixteen, and Bruhns admits that she won't take anyone under eighteen. She does, however, have suggestions for teenagers who would like to go on digs before they reach college. "There are a number of excavations in Israel and England that will take volunteers, but they prefer students with some experience. The easiest way to get experience is on something like Earthwatch, where you make a small donation and participate as a crew member. Your parents may look at it with less than a jaundiced eye because it doesn't cost any more than sending you to summer camp and they can take it off their taxable income. Your local university extension can probably give you the details."

Dr. Bruhns is eager to share her insights into archaeology with teenagers because she herself has found the profession rewarding. Achieving her goal of becoming an archaeologist has been more difficult for Bruhns than for most women because she met obstacles from the outset—even from within her own family. However, her struggle to overcome those obstacles has helped her to appreciate her success.

Karen Bruhns urges young people to "stand tough" too. Maybe all of them won't choose archaeology as a career, and maybe all of them won't have to "fight" as hard as she did, but she believes they should have the chance to make up their own minds about what they want to do.

Leslie E. Wildesen in her U.S. Forest Service office in Portland, Oregon, 1979

CHAPTER 4

LESLIE E. WILDESEN

PEOPLE WHO MEET Leslie Wildesen for the first time after reading her name and title on a government letterhead are apt to do a double take. The name "Leslie E. Wildesen, Ph.D." could belong either to a woman or a man, but when people see that name combined with the title "Regional Archaeologist, U.S. Forest Service," they usually assume it belongs to a man.

Once strangers have adjusted to the fact that Dr. Wildesen is a tall, smiling, mid-thirtyish woman, they usually start wondering what a government archaeologist really is. Guesses vary widely. People mispronounce the name of her profession (everything from ARCH-ol-gy to ar-KAYL-o-gy), ask her how she liked the Egyptian pyramids (she's never seen them), assume she knows everything about Louis B. Leakey's paleontological expeditions to East Africa (she doesn't), and even introduce her as someone "who constructs government bridges" (archaeologists almost never construct bridges and rarely excavate them).

If you ask Dr. Wildesen what an archaeologist really is, she will probably give you a jocular answer about someone who "likes dirt, camping, puzzles, and science fiction." If you ask her what a government archaeologist is, she will probably give you a similar answer about someone who "puts up with policy wrangles, planning committees, low salaries, and multiple copies of everything." But if you ask her exactly how she allocates her time each week as a regional archaeologist of the U.S. Forest Service, she will probably wrinkle her nose, peer at you intently through squarish metal-rimmed glasses, and give you a serious answer.

"I honestly don't know how many hours a week I spend at my profession," she says. "The official hours are easy to count, of course: forty at the Forest Service, a three-hour seminar I teach, about three or four hours preparing for the seminar, variable numbers of hours working on papers, giving lectures or preparing them, writing letters for professional societies, or simply reading to keep up with my field. However many it is, it is never enough, since I keep missing deadlines and having to cancel meetings because of conflicting schedules. I have never worked well on a rigorous clock-watching schedule; I would far rather spend a hectic few weeks of eighteen-hour days working on some special project."

Her "official" forty hours of work each week for the Forest Service are spent far away from sites where archaeological excavations are taking place. Wildesen reports at 8:30 on weekday mornings to the sixth floor of the Multnomah Building, a renovated old hotel in downtown Portland, Oregon, that now serves as a United States government office building. In a semiopen cubicle bounded on two sides by metal filing cabinets, she oversees a comprehensive archaeological program for nineteen national forests located in the states of Oregon and Washington. Mostly she works alone, though she can call upon the help of a historian who works in a room nearby as well as on the services of the office typing pool.

In other words, Wildesen no longer does archaeological research—at least not for the government. She is a full-time administrator. "Administration was never a part of my career goals," she admits, "nor a part of my university training," but she has subsequently enrolled in public administration courses on a postdoctoral level. Expecting all along to become a college professor who did archaeological field work in the summer, Wildesen did not really seek a government career, but the job at the Forest Service simply opened up for her at a time that she needed it.

Wildesen had completed her Ph.D. just one year earlier and was looking for employment in 1974 at the moment that the Forest Service was responding to a series of bills passed by the U.S. Congress requiring that artifacts and structures left by prehistoric peoples on land now owned by the federal government be studied before they were upended by dam construction, highway excavations, logging operations, and other forms of "progress."

By late 1979 the Forest Service had approximately seventy professional archaeologists including eighteen women, on its payroll. Nine of these people—among them Leslie Wildesen and Ernestene Green (see chapter 5)—held the rank of regional archaeologist, with the remainder serving in positions on the forest level. However, when Wildesen joined the Forest Service in 1974, she became the service's first archaeologist in the Pacific Northwest, its fifth Regional Archaeologist in the country, and its first woman archaeologist. This meant that she has worked with the program almost from the beginning and has helped to create much of it.

One problem she and other government archaeologists faced is the difficulty of ascertaining the presence of archaeological sites within dense tree growths. People such as loggers, who have no training in how to recognize evidence of prehistoric habitation, can cause considerable damage to artifacts, structures, and stratigraphy. Wildesen and other archaeologists therefore have had to develop regular procedures for laborers to follow when they begin logging operations in government forests. To determine what those procedures should be, Wildesen designed a project and contracted it out to free-lance archaeologists to set up and study eight artificial archaeological sites in the forests of Washington and Oregon.

Among Wildesen's most significant accomplishments has been the writing of a government guidebook about archaeology. Working eighteen hours a day and keeping a pot of coffee steaming nearby, she completed in two weeks a monumental document that has since been distributed not only to people in the Forest Service but to employees in other federal agencies, college professors, and private organizations. "Although it is no longer the only such treatise," Wildesen explains, "it was the first one to be produced, and my feedback from its users indicates that it is the most helpful and most complete." The guidebook contains information about historic as well as prehistoric sites and is not limited to archaeology in the strict sense. Nevertheless, she counts it as a major contribution to her profession. The guidebook was so successful that in 1979 she updated and expanded its material for a second edition.

Despite the recognition she has received, Wildesen is restless working as a bureaucrat and longs to be doing archaeological research in the field. "The single most frustrating thing about my current position," she admits, "is that there is no end product."

Although she helped to develop from the ground up a program of cultural resources management involving twenty-four million acres of federal land, she bewails the fact that "there is nothing specific I can point to, or hold in my hand, that constitutes a contribution; all I can show for the last few years are my pay stubs, larger figures on a budget printout, and a bunch of dots on maps which represent sites which have been located and protected."

Acknowledging that some people enjoy administration and that she herself has learned a great deal while working for the government, she lacks the optimism toward government archaeology that Ernestene Green expresses and Wildesen looks forward to the time when she can return to a traditional career in teaching and field work. Meanwhile, she admits that she has come this far in her career because she has encountered a string of lucky accidents.

Not all of her accidents have been lucky ones, however. By conventional standards, the first accident in her life was a bad one: Her parents divorced several months after her birth.

Leslie Elizabeth Wildesen was born during World War II on December 5, 1944, to Jane Wildesen Allstrom and her husband Allan, who had recently been discharged from the U.S. Navy. When the couple divorced, Mrs. Allstrom deposited Leslie with her own mother to be cared for ("My mother didn't like children much, especially me," Wildesen says with no rancor) while she proceeded to make a new life for herself as a single woman.

Wildesen's maternal grandmother, Frances Hills, accepted the infant good naturedly, though not without some definite ideas about child rearing. Born in the East and educated at highly-touted finishing schools, Mrs. Hills hated the West, to which she had reluctantly moved after a divorce from her husband because doctors thought the dry climate in Phoenix, Arizona, would be soothing to her asthma. Thus she was determined to give tiny Leslie a "ladylike" Eastern upbringing, emphasizing such things as correct language, appropriate dress, and the proper ways to entertain guests. As a child Leslie therefore had little experience in the outdoors. She never went hunting, fishing, or camping. And unlike most children in Arizona (certainly the ones who grow up to be archaeologists!) she never looked for arrow heads, never collected shards, and never visited any Indian dwellings—past or present.

Early in her life Leslie experienced another event that most

Leslie Wildesen and her grandmother Frances Hills in Phoenix, Arizona, 1947

people would consider unfortunate but that she recalls with an almost perverse pleasure. At age four she developed rheumatic fever—an illness that caused her little physical discomfort but that confined her to bed or a wheelchair for the next six years. Thereafter Grandmother Hills became more protective than ever, always making herself available to read the child stories, teach her math tables, or join her in quiet games.

When penicillin was discovered, the drug cured her illness and made it possible for her to go to school with other children in the middle of the fifth grade. By that time Leslie had been so well-tutored at home that she was far ahead of the other students in most academic subjects. However, her early years as a sickly and overprotected child left two lasting effects on her life. For one thing, she has never developed any interest in active physical sports. She was excused (at her grandmother's request) from physical education during high school and took only two quarters of golf in college. Today her favorite activities are those that she can do sitting down—gardening, reading, and bicycling.

For another thing, she has developed different attitudes toward archaeology from those held by people who became interested in artifacts like arrow heads and potsherds when they were children. As Wildesen herself explains, "I suspect that my attraction for theory, sediments, paleoenvironments, and recently for policymaking, stems from this initial nonattraction for the artifacts themselves. For me, artifacts may have beauty, or may reveal information upon careful analysis, but without their context they do not have intrinsic value as objects of scientific research."

Being reared by an overly protective grandmother was a "neat" experience for Leslie only until she turned sixteen. Then her high school friends started receiving their own cars, and Leslie felt like a social disaster because she always had to beg rides from her friends and could never return the favor. To Leslie and her classmates, cars were an important extension of their own personalities, and not owning one was a painful deprivation. Being two generations removed, Leslie's grandmother could not understand that. Mrs. Hills, who seldom ventured farther from home than the neighborhood grocery store, regarded automobiles as foolish luxuries that people could live without if they would just put their minds to it—certainly not playthings to be entrusted to teenagers. As a result, tempers flared once or twice over the issue, but Mrs. Hills stood firm. Not until Leslie was twenty-three years old and had graduated from college did her grandmother relent sufficiently to fix up her own twelve-year-old Pontiac to give to the younger woman.

When she wasn't moping about her lack of "wheels," Leslie spent much of her free time during her teens walking to the library to check out books on Troy, Egypt, and other exotic ancient civilizations. As a younger child she had read Richard Halliburton's adventure essays, but as she reports, "All of these books seemed to me like fairy tales, similar to *Winnie the Pooh* or the Oz books. I did not become attracted to archaeology per se during this time, but rather to the notion of escape from the everyday world, and to the possibility of discovering something no one has ever seen before in modern times."

Meanwhile, she was preparing to major in the hard sciences in college. She took advanced-placement math, including calculus, for four years, and participated in statewide mathematics competitions. She also edited the literary magazine, took advanced-placement English and history, and puttered around in photographic darkrooms.

The decision about which university she would go to had already been made. Grandmother Hills had selected Stanford for two reasons. First, it was an excellent place to meet a husband. Second, Leslie herself would have a good education if her husband were to die before she did. Having lost three husbands herself, Frances Hills was practical about the possibility of widowhood.

Another element of her grandmother's carefully wrought design for Leslie's future was that Leslie (whom the older woman still treated like a semiinvalid) wouldn't have to jeopardize either her grades or her health by working before she graduated from college. Instead, Mrs. Hills sold some rental property she had acquired from one of her husbands' estates and thereby supplemented the partial scholarship and student loan Leslie had received from Stanford. As a result of her grandmother's sacrifice, Leslie didn't have to work while she attended Stanford during the next four years—not even in the summers.

Once she was situated on the university campus, just a few miles south of San Francisco, Wildesen recalls that she "agonized over a choice of majors. My primary goal at that time was, as clearly as I could picture it, to write nonfiction on a free-lance basis." However, no college major precisely fit that ambition. She found journalism to be academically distasteful and the sciences to be socially dull. As a compromise she settled on English and philosophy, with no clear career plans in mind.

"During my senior year," she recalls, "a friend suggested that I complete my social science requirement by enrolling in an introduction to anthropology course; it sounded interesting, so I did. I found it boring because the professor tried so hard to convince me of what already was self-evident—that other cultures are different, that each culture has value, that cultures develop and change through time, and that, if you know how to listen, even the stones can speak." The films shown in the class were so insulting—both to Leslie's intelligence and to the integrity of the cultures depicted—that by the time the course ended she had decided on a new goal in life: to make *good* ethnographic films some day to replace the dreadful ones she had watched in class.

To do this meant that she would have to change her previous plans for graduate school. She had already been accepted into a midwestern university to work toward an M.A. in creative writing, but she abruptly applied for admission to nearby San Francisco State University for a double major in communications and anthropology. When the fall term began at San Francisco, Leslie enrolled in anthropology courses to fill the gaps in her undergraduate training, but before she could take a filmmaking class, another accident in her life sent her career in a still different direction. Registered for a course in primitive technology, she went to her professor's office to ask her a question, but her professor referred Leslie down the hall to the people in "the lab." As Wildesen explains, "I entered 'the lab,' got my question answered, and almost literally never left it again for three more years. The 'lab' had bones and stones to catalog, measure, and analyze; soil samples to examine; a bottomless coffee pot to drink from; and a group of students and faculty to join in salvage archaeology projects on weekends and during summer vacations. I was *home*, and that was how I felt—and still feel—about archaeology."

Thus Wildesen concludes that she did not choose archaeology as a career but rather stumbled upon it. "It seemed to fit my interests, and perhaps I had been preparing for it with my reading, studies, and desire to do something new rather than simply to repeat what others had already discovered."

Despite her sudden awareness of who she was and what she wanted in life, her old friends were beginning to view her with curiosity. Her women friends from Stanford were by then either married or typing letters in San Francisco business offices for three hundred dollars a month. Her male friends from Stanford were working as management trainees for eight hundred dollars a month. It never occurred to Leslie at the time to wonder why there was such a discrepancy in the salaries and titles of her female and male friends—possibly because she was too busy trying to deal with their thinly-veiled suspicion that she was "weird" for choosing to go to graduate school to study anthropology.

Somewhat ill at ease among her former college associates, Leslie volunteered more and more frequently to join her new friends from

San Francisco State University on salvage archaeology projects. California was experiencing what Wildesen now refers to as a "logarithmic increase in highway and other development," and students from many universities in the state were attempting to coordinate their unpaid salvage work. "Our university," she recalls, "developed a cadre of students who had more heart than brains, and who would work long hours for free, surveying, excavating, analyzing, and publishing the results of their field work in archaeology."

As one of the brightest and most zealous of the San Francisco State volunteers, Leslie was named director of a particular project to excavate a prehistoric cemetery located at a spot destined for the construction of a suburban shopping mall. Under a contract that indicated the date that the archaeological investigations would end and the bulldozers would start to roll, the private land developer donated to the American Indian Historical Society five thousand dollars, which the society then granted to Leslie and her associates toward their expenses. It was her first experience as a project director, and she now recalls it as an "archaeological success but an administrative disaster." Her biggest problem as an unmarried twenty-four-year-old female graduate student was in knowing how to deal with a macho thirty-five-year-old male undergraduate "who thought he knew everything."

Another uncomfortable situation developed for Leslie that summer. Before that time her grandmother had given Leslie her wholehearted support about graduate school—no doubt because Grandmother Hills did not really understand what Leslie was doing and was caught up in romantic misconceptions that archaeology was a profession people conducted at sherry parties or on trips to Egypt with lots of servants. When Frances Hills finally visited Leslie on her archaeological dig in 1969, she was so offended by the "filthy" men (they had dirt under their fingernails and dust on their shaggy beards) and "naked" women (they were wearing shorts and halters to dig in the hot sun) that she refused to get out of the car. Thereafter she continued to send Leslie newspaper clippings about archaeology elsewhere but avoided asking her granddaughter any questions about what she was doing.

While at San Francisco State, Leslie realized that her own particular interest in archaeology was geologic—that is, she was

Leslie Wildesen *Photo by Wilbur Gregg*

more interested in the soil conditions that invited habitation at a given spot than in the artifacts and structures the early peoples had left behind. She wrote her M.A. thesis, "Temporal and Areal Relations in Alameda County, California," after three years in residence and intended to stay in the San Francisco area for a similar period while she completed her Ph.D. Then suddenly her curiosity about something she discovered at an archaeological site in 1970 caused her to formulate other plans.

As she explains, "The site I had been digging had something 'funny' going on in the soils; I didn't know what, so I asked a friend of mine who was a soil scientist to come out one weekend and take a look. He told me that the soil at my site was a 'silt loan,' which made no sense to me and somehow didn't really answer my questions. Hence, when another friend showed me a university catalog that included courses in soils, paleoenvironments, and so forth, I rented out my apartment, quit my job, packed my things, and headed off to Pullman, Washington, wherever *that* was."

At Washington State University in Pullman, Leslie soon met Roald Fryxell and Richard Daugherty, who were to become very important in her subsequent training. Dr. Fryxell was a geologist who was teaching on the anthropology faculty and conducting exactly the kind of investigations that interested Leslie. She became Fryxell's research assistant in the university laboratory and accompanied Dr. Daugherty, an archaeologist, to a field school at the Ozette site in the summer of 1971—her first important job as a "professional" archaeologist. There her duties included supervising the training of archaeology students in exposing and interpreting stratigraphy of the soil.

Ozette proved to be the most fascinating spot she had ever visited. Once occupied by ancestors of the whale-hunting Makah Indians, this village had been under excavation by archaeologists from Washington State University for four years when they made a remarkable discovery in 1970. With the help of contemporary Makah Indians, Dr. Daugherty learned that a portion of the village had been buried hundreds of years earlier by mud slides that had blanketed several houses and hardened into an airtight seal. Artifacts from organic materials (such as wooden carvings, baskets, and bone harpoons) were therefore protected from decay in much the same manner that objects in the city of Pompeii were preserved by the volcanic ash that erupted from Mt. Vesuvius. In 1971, when Leslie joined the Ozette project, incredible recoveries from this prehistoric site were excavated and recorded, giving scientists far more information about an ancient Indian culture in the American Northwest than had ever been known before.

Like all archaeological digs, however, Ozette had its tedious aspects. Leslie soon discovered that one of her main responsibilities was to go to town once a week for oil. This required hiking four miles to a car parked at the trail head and then driving twenty miles to town over a road so full of chuckholes that the automobile trip took a full hour.

Furthermore, crew members were expected to work rain or shine (usually rain) seven days a week. Their only recreation consisted of nightly wine and song parties, with accompaniment provided by two guitars and a recorder. Since Leslie had been one of the two guitarists resourceful enough to bring her instrument along, the crew members frequently congregated in her quarters for their entertainment. In her tiny (eight by seven feet) cabin, which also held a desk, a bed, a potbellied stove, and a foot locker, she once counted seventeen guests.

Returning to Pullman in September, Leslie taught introductory courses in the anthropology department of Washington State University while she completed work for her Ph.D. The latter task took her until 1973 when she was twenty-eight years old—slightly longer than usual because she had changed specialties and universities in the interim. At last armed with the doctorate that gave her the credentials of a full-fledged archaeologist, she began the sometimes disheartening and sometimes humorous process of looking for permanent employment.

Several anthropology departments seemed interested in the curriculum vitae she mailed them and offered her plane fare to visit their campuses. But when she arrived for her interviews she somehow got the feeling that the faculties were responding to affirmative action demands to hire a woman—any woman—and were not really looking for an archaeologist. The question she was usually asked was "Would you be willing to teach a course in women's studies?" and when she truthfully answered that she would have to study the subject before she could teach it, she was not hired.

She finally landed a job at the University of California at Riverside through the help of a fellow student (male) she had known some years earlier at San Francisco State. The position was labeled "senior research assistant" on an archaeological contract—a title that proved to be a euphemism for the herculean task of teaching three courses plus working full time as the supervisor of a staff of fifty people. The best thing about it was that the job gave her the opportunity to help with some field work at Calico in the Mohave Desert.

Leslie Wildesen, right, at Manis Mastodon site, 1977

"Calico," Wildesen confesses, "excites me because it is so enigmatic. Respected professional archaeologists and geologists violently disagree on how to interpret the materials recovered from Calico. Some claim that the site contains evidence that humans were living there half a million years ago; some claim there is no evidence of humans at all; some claim that the site is only a few thousand years old." In any event, over a fifteen-year period, the site has been painstakingly excavated with dental picks, reaching a depth of almost fifty feet. As Wildesen explains, "The site was chosen for study on the recommendation of Louis B. Leakey of East African fame, and the very *least* that it provides is the most complete picture of a massive alluvial fan anywhere in the world."

Other prerequisites of her position at Riverside were that it gave her entrée into the local lecture circuit, provided visibility for

Leslie Wildesen taking a rubbing from an Indian petroglyph

outside consulting jobs, and lent credibility to her appearances before the local planning commission. As it turned out, however, the job offered her too many opportunities—more than she could handle. She was overworked, underpaid, and undersupported—at least by her department chairman. Trying to maintain high standards in the classroom, Wildesen would not give A's or B's to students who had not earned them, so indignant males were always appealing to the faculty administration to have their grades changed. "By spring," she recalls, "I had had it, and I sent my vita up the flagpole in search of another job."

All the openings at other universities seemed too similar to the position Wildesen was leaving, so when the Forest Service offered her a chance to go to Portland, she was really intrigued. For one thing, the job had just been created, and she would have the opportunity to develop a new program in her own way. For

Dr. Wildesen, left, and her assistant, Mrs. Gail Throop, recording a historic building for a Forest Service inventory

another thing, her office would be in the Northwest, a region that she had grown to love during her stint at Washington State University. She therefore snatched the government offer—but only on condition that she could remain in California long enough to complete her summer field work.

When she reached Portland in the fall, her first reaction was that there was no sex discrimination within offices in the federal government. "Being female is an asset in initial hiring," she reports, "because of the emphasis placed on equal opportunity." As she settled into her job, however, her perceptions changed, particularly after she was appointed Chair of the Committee on the Status of Women in Archaeology of the Society for American Archaeology in 1978. "The more information I learn, and the further along the path from 'recent Ph.D.' to 'grand old *man*' of the profession I get, the more incensed I become at the diminished expectations women are led to have, and at the decreased opportunities women are offered to fulfill even those expectations," she says. Within the Forest Service, men have considerable mobility, moving with apparent ease from one division to another, whereas women are kept in their original offices, usually with curbs on advancement. Wildesen has also experienced a more subtle kind of discrimination. She complains that her supervisors often pile extra work on her because they assume that as a single woman she has no personal life—an assumption they do not make regarding the single men in the office.

These problems have weighed increasingly upon her during the past few years, giving her some doubts about the long-range opportunities that government service can offer her. More importantly, Wildesen feels she has now completed the work she was hired to do in 1974—to develop an archaeological program for the nineteen national forests in Washington and Oregon—and she is restless to move on. Federal service is a twelve-month job, leaving no time for field work, so she would like to teach at a university, where she would have her summers off to conduct original research.

Although she has been a pioneer among women archaeologists in the federal government, perhaps by the time you read this biography the name "Leslie E. Wildesen, Ph.D." will no longer be combined with the title "Regional Archaeologist, U.S. Forest Service."

Leslie Wildesen *Photo by Barbara Williams*

Ernestene Green labels material in the laboratory

CHAPTER 5

ERNESTENE (DEEDEE) GREEN

"I'VE JUST NEVER allowed myself to become discouraged," explains Ernestene Green in summing up her career as an archaeologist.

Among problems that might easily have sidetracked a less tough-minded person is a recent one Dr. Green faced. In order to accept a promotion to Regional Archaeologist in a different region of the United States Forest Service, she had to move from Atlanta, Georgia, to Missoula, Montana, setting up housekeeping more than two thousand miles away from her husband. By the time she was confronting that problem in the spring of 1979, however, Dr. Green was accustomed to making difficult decisions and traveling to far-off places by herself. Pursuing her teenage dream of becoming a topnotch archaeologist had required her to leapfrog along a career path that started in Texas and took her through Arizona, Hawaii, Thailand, Pennsylvania, Guatemala, Michigan, New Mexico, and Georgia before she finally landed in Montana.

DeeDee (as she was nicknamed) Green was born in Cameron, Texas, on December 28, 1939. Her self-confidence in school, which eventually led to confidence in her career, began when she was about nine years old. That was when she asked her father to teach her to play baseball so the other kids at school would want her to be on their teams. She went outside with her father, who worked with her patiently until at last she could catch, throw, and hit a baseball. The first time she showed off her new skills at school, knocking a ball to center field, the other kids were dumbfounded and clamored to have her on their teams. This change in their attitudes toward her not only boosted her confidence at recess time but in the classroom as well. Soon she was bringing home papers with A's instead of C's, and DeeDee developed the self-assurance and equanimity that are her hallmarks today.

DeeDee's parents (J. Nelson Green, an insurance claims adjuster, and LaVerne Green, a housewife and secretary) had faith in their daughter from the beginning, of course. "Both my mother and father were significant influences in my life," Green notes. Always believing she could succeed at anything if she just tried hard enough, they included college and a professional career in their goals for her. "My father had his degree in law and often spoke of his university experiences. I realized all my life that I was expected to go to college too."

Being an only child, DeeDee was also the focus of her family's social activities, and her parents included her in most of their trips and outings. In particular she recalls the summer visits the family took to see her mother's friends who lived on a ranch near Santa Fe, New Mexico. DeeDee anticipated those trips for weeks, knowing that she would be able to spend long hours on horseback, riding back and forth from the barn to the road. Eventually her father bought one of the ranch horses to take back to Texas for use with the sheriff's posse in Lubbock, where the Greens were then living.

Besides horseback riding, the trips to New Mexico provided opportunities for DeeDee to enjoy another favorite pastime: visiting the Indian pueblos she read about in *New Mexico* magazine. Addicted to poring over that magazine, she never suspected there was such a career as archaeology, much less that she could grow up to get paid for doing the one thing she loved doing most—learning about Indians.

Expressing a desire to learn about Indians is likely to be answered with a practical suggestion in the Southwest. As soon as DeeDee mentioned that wish in Amarillo (one of several Texas cities where the Green family lived), someone recommended that she visit the Panhandle-Plains Historical Museum in Canyon, Texas, just twenty miles away. The next Saturday DeeDee rounded up a few other girls from her high school and made the trip to Canyon. It wasn't the longest trip she would ever take, but it was probably the most important: on it she met Jack T. Hughes.

Dr. Hughes, an assistant curator for the museum, was the first professional archaeologist Ernestene Green ever talked to, and she was fascinated by him. A warm, relaxed person, Hughes was eager to answer any questions that visitors to the museum might ask, and DeeDee Green was full of questions. Before that first Saturday discussion had ended, Hughes had given her a short college course on the history of the Plains Indians, and she had volunteered to return every Saturday to do odd jobs for him, bringing her girl friends with her.

Hughes always managed to create interesting assignments to keep his "assistants" busy and was generous in sharing his own time with them. Coffee breaks were the highlights of the day because Hughes would sit down with the girls and talk to them about artifacts while he sipped his coke or coffee. Using paper napkins from the dispenser, he would make sketches as he talked, drawing the cross sections of various artifacts or illustrating how one object was related to something else. "He got me thinking about the associations and contexts of things," Green reflects. "It was an informal way of teaching, and I had no idea at the time that I was learning as much as I was. But I was picking up the mind set, the mental approach that is important in archaeology."

Weather permitting, Hughes took the girls outdoors to excavate, showing them how to feel the strata with their trowels as well as how to differentiate the layers of soil with their eyes. "I made a lot of mistakes," Green recalls. "Amateurs never seem to understand that stratigraphy is complex, and their first inclination is to try to even everything out in horizontal layers. But Jack was very patient with us. He really wanted to teach us how to do things right."

Before she realized it, DeeDee was so hooked on her lifestyle as an amateur archaeologist that she seemed to be living from one Saturday until the next, when she could go digging again. "I remember one weekend," she says. "We had been excavating for about two months in just beautiful weather when suddenly it rained and rained and rained. I was afraid that the rain would ruin the site, and I was so disappointed that we couldn't go digging that I paced up and down the living room all day."

DeeDee was undoubtedly the most enthusiastic of Jack Hughes's volunteers, but several of her girl friends went to Canyon with her nearly every Saturday for two years. In the summers they excavated and in the winters they did lab work in the basement of the museum. For one particular laboratory job they were asked to separate the bones of several individuals that had been uncovered the previous summer, jumbled together in mass burial sites. Hughes explained how to tell a left bone from a right and how to determine, by their general weight and size, if particular bones came from the same individual. With the benefit of hindsight Green realizes that Jack Hughes taught her a great deal about anatomy as well as about field and museum techniques, but at the time she only knew she was having fun.

Although she had talents and interests in other fields also—art and economics to name two—nothing seemed as important to high school senior Ernestene Green as going to college and studying to become an archaeologist. The big question in her mind was which university to attend. Jack Hughes suggested she return to her former hometown of Lubbock, about a hundred miles south of Amarillo, to study at Texas Tech under Fred Wendorf. The idea was warmly received in the Green household, and DeeDee's father drove her to college, taking the trouble to visit Dr. Wendorf in his office and to introduce himself and his daughter.

Even so, Wendorf was not prepared for the fact that he had such an outstanding young student on his hands. In addition to her many talents and natural curiosity, her previous association with Jack Hughes had been "a tremendous learning experience." As Green now modestly admits, "I went to college with a great deal more knowledge than any of my fellow students."

Wendorf treated her like the other undergraduates for the first year. She sat beside them in classes, absorbing the academic and philosophical concepts to reinforce her previous field experience. She also excavated beside them the following summer at Fort Burgwin, near Taos, New Mexico, listening dutifully as Wendorf explained the techniques she had already learned from Jack Hughes.

The second year, however, things changed. DeeDee's superiority over her classmates was more widely acknowledged and Wendorf asked her, a female student who had completed only her sophomore year of college, to take charge of part of the excavation, supervising a crew of four male workers. Once again Green is modest in discussing that assignment, noting only that "it gave me a chance to learn how to operate a backhoe, which is something that women seldom do."

As much as she enjoyed Fred Wendorf's classes and as grateful as she was for the opportunities he had given her, DeeDee decided after her sophomore year that it was time to move on. The anthropology department at Texas Tech was progressing skittishly as it tried to establish an identity apart from that of the history department, and DeeDee wanted to get her B.A. degree from a more prestigious institution. She therefore applied to the University of Arizona at Tucson for the fall 1959 term.

At Arizona DeeDee painfully realized that she still had a great deal to learn about the world and felt challenged for the first time since she had conquered baseball in the fourth grade. Her most unremitting challenger was Ray Thompson, an Easterner and Harvard graduate who seemed determined to educate DeeDee in grammar and diction as well as in archaeology. "Coming from Texas," she recalls, "I spoke a different kind of language than Ray did, and he tried to improve my accent by always pointing it out to me when I made a mistake. He was even more demanding on the papers I wrote and read everything very carefully so he could indicate every word I had misspelled. I thank him for it now, but it was very hard on me when I was a student."

The problem no doubt seemed more important than it was because DeeDee allowed herself so few diversions in those days. Relentlessly trying to stay at the top of her class and to learn everything she possibly could about archaeology, she devoted all her energy to study, spending very little time on things like television, dates, hobbies, and exercise. Today a sailboat owner and regular jogger, Green opines, "I should at least have started jogging when I was in college. I think it would have helped me mentally as well as physically."

The following June allowed her the opportunity of expanding her field experience by studying in summer field school under Dr. Thompson. At Point of Pines Field School maintained by the University of Arizona, Thompson now at least *looked* different. Instead of a coat and tie, he wore khakis and tied a red bandana around his bald head (to keep the sun out of his eyes, he explained). He also gave the appearance of a relaxed family man as he sat at meals with his wife and two daughters or stooped down to pet his dachshund, which followed him about the excavation. With students, however, he was as demanding as ever, carefully checking their work and pointing out all mistakes. Off duty he maintained an equally tight ship. For Saturday night "relaxation," he organized and directed square dancing.

Thompson was so unlike anyone whom DeeDee had ever known that he alternately baffled and intrigued her. Striving to meet his high expectations, she was often frustrated, but her overall experience as an undergraduate student was mind stretching and eminently worthwhile. She was elected to Sigma Xi honor society, and after receiving her B.A. in 1961, she chose to remain at Arizona to continue studying under Thompson for her M.A. in archaeology.

In 1962 the University of Arizona opened another archaeological field school at Grasshopper, near Point of Pines. DeeDee was among the small staff that went to the site a few weeks early to erect the facilities—such things as sleeping quarters, dining hall, laboratory, and latrines. She helped with the basic carpentry, but mostly she supervised internal arrangements in the lab. This followed the common pattern of the times. Women were hired as lab assistants at archaeological digs while the men became excavation foremen. Sexism notwithstanding, she learned a great deal about constructing field camps—information she would find useful on many subsequent occasions—and she had a good time in the process.

DeeDee's equanimity got her through other problems in graduate school. Sexual discrimination was more noticeable on field trips than in the classroom, but she encountered several professors and male students who tried to discourage her from working so hard in school on the grounds that she would "just get married and give up archaeology anyway." On the whole, however, she was probably taunted less than the other female students were, simply because she was so imperturbable.

Meanwhile, she was honing a new skill. Since early childhood she had been exposed to art (her grandmother was an amateur artist who kept her home filled with paints and finished canvases), and DeeDee had demonstrated a definite talent for it. This special aptitude, plus her interest in archaeology, led her to enroll in a course in scientific illustration offered by the biology department at Arizona. Under the tutelage of "a very nice professional illustrator who somehow wound up teaching at a university," she received "fatherly" instruction in the techniques of illustrating scientific reports.

Unlike her previous art training, which had emphasized impression, composition, and color, scientific illustration seemed to focus primarily on accuracy. DeeDee loved the course and demonstrated such talent in rendering artifacts precisely that she was invited to serve as a teaching assistant in scientific illustration after she had completed the course herself. Later she did her own artwork for her thesis, which she submitted in time to receive her M.A. degree from Arizona in June 1963.

Armed with two degrees from the same institution, DeeDee decided to broaden her training by enrolling for further graduate study at the University of Hawaii under Wilhelm G. (Bill) Solheim, one of the few American professors who specialized in the archaeology of Southeast Asia. She had attended classes in Hawaii for several months when Solheim asked her if she would like to go to Thailand for nine months to work on a project he was supervising.

Back home in Texas, Nelson and LaVerne Green were excited about their daughter's projected trip to Thailand and started befriending a number of young air force men from that country who were stationed at a base near Amarillo under a military exchange program. They invited the young airmen to dinner and showed them the sights of Amarillo while they pumped the men for the kinds of information they thought would be helpful to DeeDee.

The Greens became particularly attached to one of the young Thais, treating him almost like a son. As luck would have it, he was transferred back to Bangkok before DeeDee arrived in Thailand all alone, so he was able to meet her at the airport and to provide the same kind of hospitality for her that her parents had given him in America. Working in conjunction with the National Museum in Thailand she rounded up a truck, a truck driver, and a Thai archaeology student to assist her with her research. After several weeks in Bangkok and after hiring the rest of her crew, DeeDee

Ernestene Green

embarked on her mission, faced with the responsibility of conducting scientific research in the hinterlands of a strange country assisted by four males who spoke a totally different language.

Off they drove in the fifteen-ton Dodge, DeeDee, wedged into the cab between her chief assistant and the driver, while the other two crew members straddled the equipment in the bed of the truck. "We really were a sight," she recalls, "and it must have been very uncomfortable for the ones riding in back. The roads were dirt paths used mainly by pedestrians and ox carts. Only rarely did you see a car trying to get through those potholes."

Their destination was the Korat plateau in northeastern Thailand, an area in which very little archaeological work had ever been done. Bill Solheim, however, theorized that in that area the rivers, which are tributaries of the Mekong, would prove to be part of a major transportation system dating back to prehistoric times. He had found archaeological sites along their banks, and DeeDee's job was to test them.

En route to the Korat plateau, DeeDee was obliged to arrange nightly sleeping accommodations for herself and her crew. Fortunately, one of her crew spoke some English, so by uttering simple words in English, she was able to communicate her wishes, which the Thai then translated to the villagers. "I can assure you that there weren't any motels in the places we traveled," Green reports, "so we were always on the lookout for the Buddhist wats. It's traditional in Buddhist countries that travelers who have no other place to stay can go to the wats." According to DeeDee, wats are religious compounds that usually include a structure built especially for visitors. The main difference between a Buddhist wat in Thailand and, say, a compound of Catholic buildings in America is that the buildings in the wat are erected on three-foot-high poles for protection in the event of rain. They are also completely open sided, having no walls, doors, or windows, but only a platform and a thatched roof.

As the only woman among her crew (and often the only woman in the wat) DeeDee had to learn how to dress and undress under a sarong, a piece of cloth that covers the body from chest to knees. "There's a real trick to it," she says, "and I don't think I could do it any more. But you learn the technique of putting certain items of clothing on first over your head and then taking off your jeans from underneath." She also learned the technique of taking a shower. "You try to soap yourself down underneath the sarong," she explains, "and then you splash yourself with a cup of water. Amazingly enough, you can get pretty clean that way."

In addition to being the only woman in some of the places where she stayed, DeeDee was usually the only Caucasian. She therefore attracted considerable curiosity among villagers she encountered who had never before seen an Anglo of either sex. On one occasion, after Bill Solheim and his wife had come to join her, Green was doing some mending in a small village where a religious festival was taking place. The spectators for the ceremony, however, were much more intrigued by DeeDee and Mrs. Solheim than they were by the festival, and they stood and watched the two white women sew while the religious performance continued.

DeeDee's archaeological activities caused further suspicions among the natives, particularly the ones who still believed in the ancient spirit religion, or animism, rather than the more modern Buddhism. As Green explains, "Buddhism is relatively recent in comparison to animism, which is a belief in things like souls, ghosts, and demons." A local shaman, or practitioner of black magic arts, placed a curse on DeeDee and Bill Solheim for disturbing the natural world by excavating it. "He said both Bill and I would die within a month. That was about twelve years ago."

A second curse was placed on her that she didn't learn about until after she had escaped from it. She and her crew had received permission to dig in a Buddhist wat to excavate a circle of stones that had had religious significance in ancient times. The stones were of no importance to the Buddhists, who objected to the contemporary belief in animism, so they were happy to help the archaeologists in whatever ways they could. DeeDee noticed that each day some women would come to the wat and place rice on the stones, as a gift to the spirits. When dogs came along behind the women and ate the rice, the superstitious villagers said the dogs were eating the rice on behalf of the spirits. At any rate, a shaman apparently objected to the archaeologists' tampering with the sacred stones and put a curse on DeeDee's newly acquired Land Rover, claiming it wouldn't start if DeeDee tried to pack up and leave. As DeeDee turned the ignition and the engine responded, her assistant sitting next to her let out a great sigh. Only then did he tell her about the shaman's curse.

DeeDee was excavating in Thailand during the Vietnamese War. Serene as always, she had paid little attention to news of the violence taking place nearby until Bill Solheim's visit heightened her awareness about her own possible danger. He had a better sense of what was going on and cautioned her to be watchful for signs indicating that she should escape the country. "We talked about various contingencies," she recalls, "and planned what we would do if we had to leave in a hurry." Among other things, Solheim taught her to use the motorcycle his crew had purchased the year before. "I had never been on a motorcycle and didn't know how to operate one, but I learned. I remember driving around and around the area, just practicing in case we had to get out in a hurry." Luckily she never had to use any of her carefully planned maneuvers.

Returning to the States after her stint in Thailand, DeeDee enrolled at the University of Pennsylvania and went through a strange psychological state. Except for the brief time that Bill Solheim and his wife had visited her abroad, she had been deprived of the stimulation of speaking her native language in any depth at all. For nine months she had lived and worked in the company of four Thais who spoke almost no English and with whom she communicated in a few simple English words and a few equally simple Thai words she eventually picked up. Suddenly among native English speakers again, she could talk at a normal speed, using complex phrases and grammar. At the University of Pennsylvania, she felt compelled to talk and talk, particularly about intellectual concepts. "I probably bored my fellow students in the dormitory to death," she admits.

Noted for its outstanding archaeology department, Pennsylvania was a highly competitive school with eager students and a demanding faculty. DeeDee had been in similar situations before, but none so difficult as the one at Pennsylvania. She might have found the atmosphere less challenging if she had come directly from her graduate studies at the University of Arizona; but her nine months in Thailand, where she was responsible only to herself and where she had little philosophical stimulation, put her at a disadvantage in trying to deal with a few faculty members. "I didn't know how to please some of the professors," she recalls, "so I was frustrated some of the time."

Ernestene Green anticipates a day of skiing

At that time Pennsylvania was sending many of its graduate students to Guatemala for archaeological field work, and in 1967 DeeDee went to excavate some Mayan ruins near Tikal, arriving there in one of the Guatemalan airplanes she describes as "very interesting." The planes had removable seats to accommodate any kind of load, and passengers never knew if they would share their journey with humans, chickens, pigs, or chicle, a material from a tropical evergreen tree that is used as the base for chewing gum. The entire population of Tikal, or about fifty Americans and workmen, turned out to greet the plane, since its arrival was always the biggest social event of the day. As the plane touched ground, one of DeeDee's fellow passengers made the sign of the cross and said, "Gracias a Adios," or "Thank God we arrived safely." "Given the nature of those planes," Green comments, "I kind of thought the same thing."

The actual site that DeeDee and her crew were to excavate was Navajuelal, about nine kilometers from Tikal. It was the first Mayan excavation that had ever been supervised by a woman and also the first time in the Tikal area that an excavation was so far away from the main ruins that the archaeologists had to camp during the week. Once again, DeeDee was the only woman living in primitive surroundings with a crew of men.

"We had no way to get to our site from Tikal except to walk," Green says, "and it took us half a day. We walked out Monday morning, camped there all week, and came back to Tikal Friday night." On their initial trip to Navajuelal they carried their equipment and tents on muleback. After that, they carried only food, transporting enough provisions each Monday to last the whole week.

The walks to and from the campsite were full of high adventure. "More than once I almost stumbled into a tarantula," Green reports. "I also got stung by a creature resembling a centipede that caused the most intense pain I've ever had in my life." Besides problems from insects, the hikers had to be wary of dangerous animals such as jaguars, and even of some of the bushes and trees. Growing profusely along the trail was a tree with sharp and somewhat poisonous thorns. "It's hard to walk along a jungle trail," Green notes, "and you stumble a lot, especially when you're not used to it. The natural inclination is to stick out your hand to catch hold of something, but every time you caught one of those trees, you'd get stuck with thorns that caused a painful swelling that lasted several days." After they had made that mistake a few times, they instinctively changed movement and pulled their arms in whenever they stumbled.

DeeDee was working in Guatemala during the dry season, when there was barely enough water for cooking and drinking—even less to use on luxuries like bathing. She showered only on the weekends, after her crew had walked back to Tikal from the campsite, and with a minimal amount of water. "I'd look forward to that shower during the whole walk back to Tikal on Friday afternoon," she recalls.

During the dry season the animals were as hard up for water as the archaeologists, and each noon as DeeDee and her assistants tried to relax and enjoy their sack lunches, half a dozen howler monkeys would surround them, wailing loudly. The workmen told DeeDee that the monkeys were begging for water, but she thought they were trying to run off the humans that had invaded their territory. Whatever the reason, the noise was disquieting and not at all conducive to good digestion.

On one occasion Green wanted to make some architectural drawings and climbed to a temple on top of a pyramid, a total of about thirty feet into the air. "A big male howler monkey climbed on a tree limb about five feet away from me," she says. "He stared at me eyeball-to-eyeball and started howling, but I just stared right back. By that time I had worked up my own feeling of territoriality, and it was my site. I wasn't going to let any monkeys drive us off."

Eventually the water hole by which they had camped dried up completely, and the crew had to move to another spot. This time they decided not to use tents but to occupy some champas, or open structures with thatched roofs, that had been left by workers collecting chicle for the manufacture of chewing gum. For modesty's sake, however, DeeDee's crew felt that her champa should be enclosed, so they constructed walls all the way around it, leaving only one open space for a door.

"It was like a cave inside that thing," she recalls. "I decided to take a candle inside so I could see, and that worked fine for several days. But then I made the mistake of putting the candle on a stump that ran underground. I didn't know it, but a fire started underground. About three o'clock in the morning my champa suddenly burst into flames. I ran outside and called the workmen to help put out the fire." She lost a few personal belongings, but more importantly, "the champa smelled pretty smoky for a week or two."

In addition to her own excavations at Navajuelal, DeeDee spent time on weekends with the archaeologists working in the lab at Tikal. Those episodes are among the most humorous of her experiences in Guatemala, mainly because of the resourcefulness of Dennis Puleston, another student archaeologist. When Puleston wasn't trying to get his friends to act out ancient Mayan rituals, to compare the efficiency of Mayan stone axes with modern steel ones, or to invent new recipes for using breadnuts from the ramon tree (on which Mayans may have subsisted in difficult times), he was thinking up practical jokes to play on tourists who came to visit the ruins.

With good notes from her Navajuelal excavations, DeeDee returned to Philadelphia confident that she had enough material to write her Ph.D. dissertation. She therefore concentrated on finishing up her courses at Pennsylvania and then began hunting for a permanent job. For archaeologists the process of job placement is conducted in part at the annual meeting of the American Anthropological Association, where universities or other institutions with job openings fill out forms describing their positions and applicants needing employment fill out similar forms describing their experience and qualifications. Then the applicants are interviewed by representatives from several institutions.

After six or eight brief personnel interviews at the meeting, DeeDee received letters from the institutions involved, indicating that they either did or did not want her to visit their campuses for more extensive discussions. One California institution, however, failed to notify her, so DeeDee took the initiative and wrote to the man who had interviewed her, explaining that she was setting up her travel schedule and asking if he would like to see her again.

In response, she received a warm, personal letter from the man, saying that he would very much like to see her and was looking forward to putting her up in his apartment. Nothing was mentioned about a job. Readily concluding that she was not interested in the kind of sexual exploitation his invitation implied, Green set up her interview schedule with no stops in California and eventually accepted an offer to teach at Western Michigan University in Kalamazoo.

While working her first year at Western Michigan, Green corresponded with William Coe, her dissertation adviser at Pennsylvania, about her proposed topic. But trying to communicate from a distance of one thousand miles created difficulties. She therefore decided to spend the summer of 1969 in Philadelphia so that she could talk to Coe personally and work on her dissertation under his close supervision.

Her first conference with Coe was very traumatic because she had not realized that he had been trying to tell her that she did not have enough material from Navajuelal to write a dissertation and that he wanted her to find another topic. "I guess that summer was the most difficult period of my life," she says. The first three days were especially painful, as she isolated herself, worrying how she could possibly spend the time or money to start all over again doing field research. After agonizing for seventy-two hours, she scheduled another appointment with Coe and suggested that in her paper she compare the Indians who had lived at Navajuelal to several other Mayan groups in other locations and then analyze the technique of analogy for interpreting past cultures. To her great relief, he agreed that the new topic would make an acceptable dissertation.

Green's problems with her dissertation had only begun, however. "Bill Coe did a number of wonderful things for me that I was able to appreciate later on," she says, "but at the time I had a hard time accepting all his criticism, or even understanding it. The whole summer was very difficult and frustrating, and I began to wonder if I would ever satisfy what he wanted. Many of us who had worked on the Tikal project were going through the same kind of discouragement. But partly through luck and partly by being tough-minded, I was the first one to finish."

Officially receiving her Ph.D. in June 1970, Green continued to teach at Western Michigan and for one summer ran the university's field school in New Mexico. Because that field school was located in the Cibola National Forest, she had frequent dealings with the U.S. Forest Service's Regional Archaeologist there, a man with a name that certainly made her notice him—Dee Green.

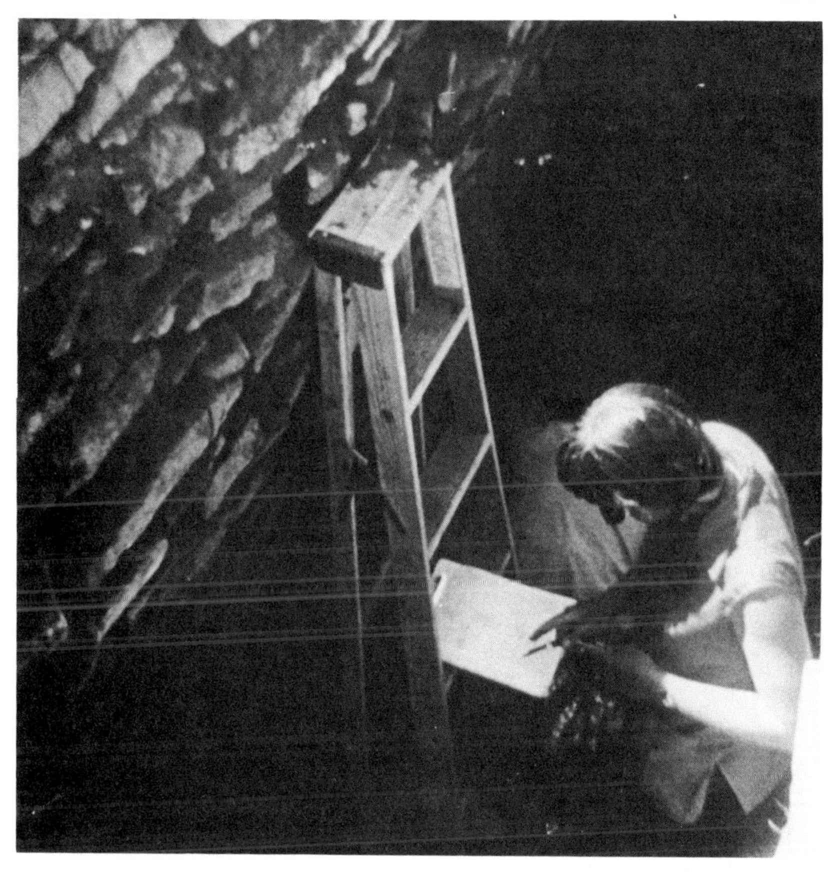

Ernestene Green records data from room of pueblo at Gallinas Spring site, New Mexico

DeeDee Green and Dee Green probably would have liked each other anyway, but their names didn't hurt their developing friendship. Thus when Dee Green heard about a job opening for an archaeologist in another region of the Forest Service, he thought of DeeDee Green. Happy with her new life in Kalamazoo, DeeDee was flattered by Dee Green's suggestion but not really tempted. Again he called her when he heard of a second job, but again she wasn't interested. When he called her the third time about a third opportunity, DeeDee decided to apply for the job.

Students from Western Michigan University listen to Dr. Green giving instructions at Gallinis Spring field school, 1974

Ernestene Green, right, watches as student adjusts camera at excavation site

As she explains it, by 1975, when she learned about the third federal opening for an archaeologist, she was teaching a course in cultural resources management—a class in which she was trying to convince her students that government archaeology would be the specialty to develop most rapidly in the next few years. A series of federal laws, beginning with the Antiquities Act of 1906, and gaining impetus after 1966, had dramatized the federal government's role in preserving our cultural heritage. Green correctly foresaw that the federal government would become the most important source of funds for archaeological research. And having urged her students to consider careers in cultural resource management, she had the feeling they were saying to her, "Well, put your money where your mouth is."

From her local civil service office, DeeDee thereupon obtained a form 171 and filled it out, with advice from Dee Green. (As a mid-level job applicant, she was not required to take a civil service test.) Her background impressed the people in personnel, and within a few months she was settled in Atlanta, across the continent from the Dee Green who had urged her to apply for the position.

When DeeDee Green joined Region 8 of the U.S. Forest Service, she was one of only a handful of women archaeologists in the national government. Like Leslie Wildesen in Oregon (chapter 4), DeeDee Green became an administrator in a federal office building, from which she traveled frequently on government business, but she no longer did any digging of her own. Her primary responsibility was to see that the archaeological program in Region 8 rolled forward in a satisfactory way. Her job therefore included handling personnel problems as they arose, supervising public relations work (such as planning brochures and television tapes), and nominating sites for the National Register of Historic Places of the Department of the Interior. Previously unfamiliar with archaeology in that part of the country, she also had to read numerous journal articles about the Southeast. "Frankly," she says, "I was so busy with the agency duties like writing memos and reading agency reports that it was hard to keep up with the professional reading."

One thing government employees don't have to read is student papers, so DeeDee's weekends became somewhat more free than they had been in the past. At first her situation of having time on the weekend as well as a little money to spend felt very strange. Gradually she realized the therapeutic value of allocating regular periods to hobbies, particularly exercise. She had to talk herself into it for a whole year but, once she started jogging, she found it really did create the highs that others had described to her. Now she is an avid jogger and also owns a sailboat that she races at every opportunity.

The sailboat gave her something in common with Rudolph Robles when he transferred to her Georgia office from California in 1977. While Rudy was visiting DeeDee's unit to meet his new coworkers, he and DeeDee discovered their mutual interest in sailing, and DeeDee invited him to crew for her. "That was an interesting role reversal," she explains. "In the sailing club I belonged to I was only the second woman to be captain of a boat. And I was the first one to have a man crewing for me."

DeeDee and Rudy were married in June 1978, and soon thereafter Rudy bought his own sailboat, competing against his wife in boat races. "Most of the time he beat me," Green admits. "But once I beat him. I talked about it so much that all the people at work thought it had happened three or four times."

Fortunately, that kind of fierce competition didn't carry over into all other aspects of their lives. Rudy was very cooperative about household duties, regularly assuming responsibilities for vacuuming rugs and fixing meals. "He'd probably tell you he did more around the house than I did," Green says candidly. As a career federal employee, he also understood his wife's responsibilities to be away from home, attending meetings in Washington, D.C., and elsewhere on the forests in the southeastern region of the United States.

Thus when DeeDee was offered the opportunity for advancement to Regional Archaeologist in the headquarters of the Northern Region in Missoula, Rudy urged her to accept. Rudy had worked for years for the Forest Service in various locations in the West and was anxious to return there himself. He immediately applied for a position in the Northern Region but decided to continue in his job in Atlanta until a suitable vacancy occurred. This meant that the couple who had been married about a year were suddenly separated for six months. Today they are reunited in Montana, where Rudy has been transferred to the civil rights unit in DeeDee's new regional office. They are happy about their decision for DeeDee to accept the promotion, even though "the six months apart were trying."

"Both of us enjoy Montana," DeeDee reports. "The countryside is lovely, and I want to learn how to cross-country ski and downhill ski. Professionally I enjoy the job here, and I recently served as the program chairperson for the 1980 annual meeting of the Society for American Archaeology."

Life as an archaeologist has worked out very well for Ernestene Green, probably because she never lets herself get discouraged.

Ernestene Green

Mary Eubanks Dunn holding Oaxacan urn encircled by cast ears of corn, 1977, at Middle American Research Institute, Tulane University *Photo by Armand Bertin*

CHAPTER 6

MARY EUBANKS DUNN

WHEN THE ATTRACTIVE woman stepped down from the podium on November 8, 1979, after reading her paper to the Southeastern Archaeological Conference, so many people rushed up to her asking for copies of her research report that she went home to Nashville, Tennessee, and had the material mimeographed for general distribution. Experiences like that are exhilarating to Mary Eubanks Dunn and reaffirm her faith that the decision she made to stick things out in archaeology was a wise one. On the whole, however, her career has been rocky.

Dr. Dunn is a young woman who only recently acquired her Ph.D., so her biography pinpoints some of the problems that today's high school and college students should anticipate if they are considering careers as archaeologists. When Dunn enrolled in graduate school, she assumed she was following the traditional path to becoming the kind of archaeologist who primarily teaches college classes, frequently conducts field work, and incidentally supervises laboratory research. What has actually happened, however, is that Dunn has become an archaeologist who primarily does laboratory research, rarely conducts field work, and incidentally teaches college classes.

As college enrollments have dropped in the past few years, fewer new people are being hired for faculty positions. Young men and women just entering the job market with Ph.D.'s are therefore finding it necessary to make compromises in order to stay in their chosen academic professions. For Dr. Dunn the compromises necessary to remain in archaeology have included (1) setting up an archaeological laboratory of her own to do free-lance work and (2) pursuing additional graduate studies in botany.

In devoting herself to scholarly pursuits, Mary Dunn is carrying on a family tradition. In an era when women were just getting the right to vote, two of her great aunts were practicing medicine. One of them—Dr. Elizabeth Bass—conducted some of the pioneering work in sickle cell anemia and was the first woman on the faculty of the Tulane University Medical School. Furthermore, as Mary Dunn explains in her rich drawl, "My father was a southern historian, and all his best friends were historians."

Her father, Michael Eubanks, had been studying toward a Ph.D. in southern history at the University of North Carolina at Chapel Hill when his wife, Nell Bass Eubanks, became so troubled with allergies in about 1950 that she had to be hospitalized for several months. Mary Dunn, who was three years old at the time, has only vague memories of her twelve-year-old sister helping her father with the cooking and cleaning while he tried to continue graduate study and provide financially for his wife and three children. Circumstances became so difficult that he postponed his plans to become a college professor and moved his family back to a small town in Mississippi, where his wife's father owned the largest pecan nursery in the world.

In that rural setting three more sons were born to Michael and Nell Eubanks, and all six of their children grew up with horses to ride and woods to roam. "My grandfather was a very wealthy man," Dunn admits, "and we were well off compared to most of the other people in the area." Nevertheless, the family had only part-time domestic help, and Mrs. Eubanks assumed most of the responsibility for canning vegetables for the winter supply and for putting up pickles and jellies. Mary had the usual share of household chores, but when they were completed she could gather any pecans that had fallen to the ground and sell them for spending money. She made a considerable amount of cash doing that, saving part of it to buy a pair of contact lenses when she was fourteen.

Mary occasionally tended the gardens or drove the tractor simply for the pleasure of doing so. More frequently, she rode through the countryside on horseback with her brothers and cousins. "I loved the outdoors," she says. "Growing up on a farm that way, outside of the city, did prepare me for archaeological field work, although ironically I don't do much actual excavation."

The pecan orchard was located in an area rich in ancient American Indian lore. Her grandfather was familiar with many Indian mounds, which he explained to the younger generation. Of particular interest to the children was a place called Indian Spring, which they believed was haunted by the spirits of Indians who had gone there to obtain drinking water.

Mary also loved to visit the home of her great-grandmother and to sit on the porch beside the old woman while her great-grandmother rocked in her chair and told stories about her Indian friends. "She had some dear, close friends who were Indians," Dr. Dunn recalls, "and her affection that was conveyed as she told me stories gave me a deep appreciation for them."

With this background from her grandfather and great-grandmother, Mary was vitally interested when her third-grade teacher began explaining about the cultures of other people, especially the Indians of North and South America. "That was my first encounter with the word *subsistence*. I remember very vividly the account in that class of the preparation of manioc by the Amazonian Indians."

In addition, Mary learned about foreign cultures through the movies her grandmother took in other countries. While her grandfather stayed home to tend his pecan nursery, Mary's grandmother traveled widely. "I was very impressed with her exploits in primitive regions and the fact that she would try just about anything," Dunn recalls. On one occasion Mary's grandmother made a trek into the mountains of Colombia, where she watched miners digging for precious stones in caves and dug out some of her own—including a very large amethyst that she brought home to Mary's mother. After each trip there were more stories to tell her grandchildren.

Mary's idyllic childhood ended and she developed broader interests when her father decided to go back to Chapel Hill, in about 1960 and resume work on his Ph.D. dissertation. For one thing, Mary won a national medal for her mystery story published in *Read* magazine. For another thing, the intelligent eighth-grader was shifting her interests from foreign countries to American government.

Inspired by her new interest in American institutions, Mary decided she wanted to become a congressional page in Washington, D.C., and conducted an intensive, though unsuccessful, campaign to become the first girl appointed to the post. When her own congressman turned her down on the grounds that the responsibilities were too difficult for a girl, Mary fired off letters like grapeshot to all the important politicians she could think of—Dwight Eisenhower, John Kennedy, Richard Nixon, and Henry Cabot Lodge, to name a few. But Mary was much too far ahead of her time, and all of the men she appealed to sent back discouraging letters. "We now have girl pages in the House and Senate," she notes with a sigh, "but being a female affected me even early in life. I think that had I been accepted as a page, I might have continued my interest in political science rather than going into archaeology later on."

Her family began having problems after they moved back to Chapel Hill. Mary's father came down with a terrible illness that hospitalized him for many months and after his release could not study or do any work. "At that time, things fell apart for our family financially," she recalls. "In spite of that, I was sent away to prep school at Abbott Academy in Andover, Massachusetts, for tenth grade." In that challenging atmosphere Mary excelled in French and English and earned higher grades in math than most of the boys in her classes. She also received such a phenomenal math score on the SAT exam that at age fifteen she was offered a full scholarship to a prestigious southern university.

It was therefore a real letdown that because of family finances (her parents couldn't afford the room and board in sending her away to college) she was compelled to go home to Chapel Hill in the eleventh grade and reenter public school. With the superior training she had received at Abbott she was far ahead of her classmates, and she was bored, bored, bored! As a result, she kept creating so much mischief that the school administrators sighed with ambivalent relief when she decided to drop out.

Her college-oriented parents were ambivalent, too. They, of course, wanted their daughter to finish high school and go to college, but they understood why she was bored, and they sympathized with her. Furthermore, an older son had once dropped out of high school, but by the time Mary made the same choice, he was a practicing lawyer. They therefore correctly assumed that Mary would eventually get her life back in order and resume her education.

Mary registered for courses at the University of North Carolina but dropped out of school a second time, deciding to travel. Taking a roundabout route through the Adirondacks and Quebec, she eventually wound up in Cambridge, Massachusetts, where she had several friends from her Abbott days, and where she found a job in a watch shop on Harvard Square. "At first I was content to be a laborer," she recalls, "but then I began to wonder what life would be like if I were still doing this when I was forty." It had been a good experience for her to realize that she could support herself away from home, but after a year she returned to Chapel Hill and at age nineteen married her first husband, Tom Settlemyre.

With a B.S. degree in psychology, Tom was working as a carpenter on big construction projects around Chapel Hill. "We were quite poor and I did a lot of work canning vegetables," she recalls. Eventually both she and Tom decided they would be better off with more education, and they registered at the university, she as an undergraduate in French and he as a graduate student in anthropology.

Together the Settlemyres took a course in art history taught by Emeline Richardson, a classical archaeologist who specialized in the Etruscan civilization. "Dr. Richardson was about sixty," Mary Dunn recalls. "She was a marvelous lecturer with tremendous poise. At age twenty I had finally come in contact with an older female whom I thought I would like to be like when I was that age." Mary was not really interested in the ancient cities of the Mediterranean, but she so admired her professor that she felt impelled to work as hard as she could in the course. Being pregnant at the time, she decided that if she got an *A* and had a girl, she would name the baby Emeline.

Somewhat disappointed when she received a B+ after working very hard in Dr. Richardson's class, Mary named her baby Dealey after a childhood friend. Later Professor Richardson told her, "You really wrote a good term paper, but you didn't do as well on the exam. That's why you made a B+ and your husband made an A."

In any event, Mary was sufficiently impressed by Dr. Richardson to take a second class from her. As soon as Dealey was old enough to leave at home, Mary returned to school, registering for the course in Etruscan civilization that was Emeline Richardson's specialty. That was a time when Dr. Richardson was in the process of borrowing valuable artifacts from all over the world for a show at the Ackland Museum in Chapel Hill called "Ancient Portraits." Dr. Richardson called upon her students to help with various tasks, and Mary became particularly involved. For her term paper she wrote catalog descriptions of some of the artifacts in the show. "It was very exciting to me," she recalls.

As a result, Mary decided to major in the classics; however, Dr. Richardson advised her that unless she wanted to stay an extra year or two in college to learn Greek (Mary had already studied French and Latin), she should select another major. Meanwhile, because she had already been influenced to take a variety of anthropology classes, Mary realized that she could graduate fairly easily in that subject.

Thus, in 1970, she received her degree in anthropology from the University of North Carolina and immediately afterward went with her husband and two other graduate students to the Dutch island of Saba in the West Indies to assist with the research for a textbook in cultural anthropology (ethnology). They took eighteen-month-old Dealey along, sharing the responsibility of caring for the baby while they managed their research. Their job was to conduct in-depth personal interviews with selected natives in order to gather information about the culture of the tiny, four-mile-wide island. Although the island was not really primitive, Saba was not industrialized either. Some of its homes had access to electricity for a few hours each night, but others did not, and many villagers did not own common household appliances like vacuum cleaners and electric mixers.

Mary established good rapport with the islanders, many of whom readily agreed to be interviewed. But when it came time for the conversations, she had a great deal of difficulty asking the probing kinds of questions that the research method required. Her own basic shyness, combined with the natives' shyness about speaking into a tape recorder, produced unsatisfactory results. "I was very insecure and immature," Dr. Dunn recalls. "I don't think I would have the same problems today." Nevertheless, the Saba experience convinced her that she wasn't cut out to do field research in cultural anthropology and that she should specialize in another aspect of anthropology for her M.A. degree.

Back at the University of North Carolina in Chapel Hill, Mary cast about for a different kind of research topic for her thesis. One day in a class on Mesoamerican archaeology, Professor Donald Brockington began describing the cylindrical funerary urns made by the Zapotec Indians of Mexico. Brockington "wrapped his lecture in an air of intrigue," explaining how an engineer who had fallen down in his luck at the turn of the century went into the business of manufacturing fake Zapotec urns and selling them to the most important museums in the world. Brockington also explained that most of the Zapotec urns bear representations of various gods—either seated, standing, or kneeling—as well as impressions of corn. Mary was so fascinated by the lecture that she decided to write her M.A. thesis on Zapotec urns, paying particular attention to the botanical motifs on them.

Soon afterward Mary was invited to a celebration given by a friend who had just passed his Ph.D. examination in anthropology. About two o'clock in the morning, as his guests were departing, the host turned to Mary and asked her what she planned to do for her M.A. thesis. When she replied that she was interested in Zapotec urns, her host became very excited. "Oh, I know just the person you have to go see." He gave her the address of Paul Mangelsdorf, who had moved to Chapel Hill after his retirement from Harvard University.

Dr. Mangelsdorf, it turned out, had been the director of the botanical museum at Harvard, and was one of the world's leading authorities on corn. He was particularly interested in representations of corn on Zapotec urns and was certain that they were impressed from molds made from actual corn ears. In other words, the urns showed exact reproductions of the prehistoric corn. Delighted to find a graduate student with a background in art and archaeology, he talked to Mary about the possibility of studying the corn on Zapotec urns. Confessing that he had spent many years looking for just the right graduate student to help him with his research, he suggested that she prepare a grant proposal describing her planned M.A. thesis and said he would recommend her for a research grant to go to Mexico to do the necessary investigations.

Accompanied by her husband and Dealey, Mary went to Mexico in 1971-1972. Traveling around the country to study pottery specimens in museums, she tried to gain a complete understanding of each urn by examining its overall dimensions and the deity represented on it. However, she was particularly concerned with the depictions of corn on these vessels and took careful measurements of each cob and kernel. Within a short time Mary learned a great deal about corn—both modern and ancient. The journey to Mexico provided her with considerable information for a fascinating M.A. thesis.

Mary's actual writing of the paper was delayed by her marital problems, however. She filed for divorce and in an effort to get a new perspective on her life and goals, she went to Europe for several weeks, traveling throughout the Continent with young Dealey. It was the first time that she had had the full care of her daughter, and Mary got a small taste of what things would be like if she ever became a professional archaeologist and had to move about frequently with a child.

As it turned out, she was forced to confront that issue sooner than she had expected. When she completed her thesis and received her master's degree in 1973, her faculty committee at Chapel Hill urged her to continue with her studies and get a Ph.D. so that she would be qualified to teach university-level classes and to supervise students in field research. In addition, the committee advised her that she should not obtain her doctor's degree from the University of North Carolina because she had obtained both her bachelor's and master's degrees from that school. Unless she broadened her training by seeking her Ph.D. at another university, she would carry the stigma of being "narrow" and "inbred" and would have difficulty finding employment as a college professor.

Mary considered her options carefully and finally applied for admission to Tulane University, which had the reputation of being one of the best universities in the world for Mesoamerican studies. Soon after her arrival in New Orleans with Dealey, she met Dr. Edward James Dunn, who was serving his surgical residency at a large hospital in that city. Mary's social life revived at once, and

Mary Dunn examining Zapotec urn at the Museo Nacional de Antropologia, Mexico City, 1972 *Photo by Tom Settlemyre*

she was married after a brief courtship, but she encountered all kinds of obstacles in her academic life.

Having chosen Tulane partly because H. Garrison Wilkes (a former student of Dr. Mangelsdorf) was on its biology faculty, Mary was distressed to learn that Dr. Wilkes had left the university very suddenly for personal reasons. She had been hoping to do an interdisciplinary dissertation in botany and anthropology, but in Wilkes's absence, there was no one at Tulane who was qualified to supervise her research. Furthermore, the tuition at Tulane was so high for the wife of a medical resident that staying there seemed pointless if she could not undertake the project she wanted to on Peruvian pottery bearing representations of corn. Mary wondered if she should give up the whole idea of studying for a Ph.D. She toyed briefly with the idea of becoming an interior decorator, but there were no schools for studying for that profession in New Orleans.

No matter what career she chose, her life would be difficult if she were to remain in New Orleans. Except for her husband, whose medical responsibilities required that he spend most of the next year traveling away from home, she had made no close friends in the city. She therefore decided to return to Chapel Hill to complete her Ph.D. under the professors who had already encouraged her research of corn representations on prehistoric urns. "That was the rational aspect of the decision," she now confesses. "But I think the real reason was that I was feeling very insecure at that time. I had doubts that I was even capable of reaching what to me was the highest level of academic achievement. I really wanted to see if I could do it."

Despite the separation from her husband, Mary now looks back on that decision as one of the best ones of her life. She completed her course work for her Ph.D. in just one year while also teaching undergraduate classes. "My mother was wonderful," Mary says. "I never had to cook or clean or worry about Dealey or anything. That was the only way I could have accomplished that amount of work with the depth of concentration that was necessary." Her husband was able to visit her occasionally in North Carolina, and altogether the year was exhilarating.

During that year of residency in Chapel Hill, Mary became pregnant with her second child, and five months after Laura

Mary Dunn displaying corn mold and ceramic cast, at her own botanical laboratory, 1977 *Photo by Armand Bertin*

Louise was born, Mary and Ed flew to South America, where Mary conducted the research for her Ph.D. dissertation. Except that she was studying ancient urns from Peru instead of Mexico, her research method was similar to the one she had used for her M.A. thesis, traveling to museums to examine and measure urns which bore representations of corn. Although museum research is less rugged than archaeological excavation, she was glad she had left her children at home with her parents. "We got into some primitive situations where we couldn't have found formula or proper medical care for the baby," she says. "The older I've grown, the more conservative I've become and the less inclined I am to take my children into the field."

Having small children has meant that Mary Dunn has done considerably less field work than most archaeologists her age, though motherhood is only one of several factors that have impeded advancement in her career. Being married to a medical doctor has also limited her mobility. Except for the one year that they maintained separate residences so she could attend school in North Carolina, she has followed Ed to the cities where his medical responsibilities have taken him.

Moreover, Mary Dunn's sex has been a serious professional handicap, and she is convinced that she was passed over for several jobs she applied for simply because she is a woman. In retrospect, she now realizes that many obstacles were placed in her path when she was in graduate school. "I wasn't sensitive to the discrimination at the time," she says, "but after I passed my Ph.D. requirements, one faculty member confided that a lot more had been demanded of me than of the male students because the faculty knew that it is difficult for a woman to get a job in archaeology. Only a woman who can demonstrate truly superior ability has a chance to make it."

Although Dunn did demonstrate superior ability all through graduate school, she subsequently spent several frustrating years trying to find paid employment as an archaeologist. Unable to obtain a job teaching or doing paid research at any of the southern universities she applied to, she was able to remain active in her profession only by serving as an unpaid research associate at various universities near her husband's work. She also did free-lance laboratory work for archaeologists who sent her materials from their field excavations.

Such assignments were infrequent, however, and when she moved to Nashville with her husband in 1978, she felt her career was at an impasse. After all the time and effort she had invested in archaeology, she could see no hope for herself in that profession. Finally she obtained a small free-lance job for the Department of Conservation, identifying plant remains from a site in Tennessee. "The significant thing about it," she relates, "was that it got me interested in going back to school to learn more botany." Through her investigations of Zapotec and Peruvian urns with clay casts of ears of corn, Mary Dunn had learned a great deal about prehistoric maize. However, she had never studied botany and did not feel adequately qualified to examine many paleobotanical materials. Furthermore, she did not own the laboratory equipment for certain paleobotanical techniques.

Dr. Dunn collecting plants at site of ancient Indian mound in Bayou des Coquilles, Jefferson Parish, Louisiana, 1978 *Photo by L. Lawrence Beavers*

With nine-year-old Dealey in school and two-year-old Laura Louise old enough to go to nursery school, Dr. Dunn decided to return to school once more. After some difficulty she managed to get a special scholarship and enrolled at Vanderbilt University in Nashville to do graduate work in botany. At first the new routine was difficult. In addition to having to adjust to more difficult family schedules, Dr. Dunn had to get back into the habit of studying and taking exams. She also felt ill at ease among the other, younger, graduate students most of whom had received bachelor's degrees in biology and were better prepared for the graduate botany classes than she was.

Concluding that she had made a mistake, Mary Dunn confessed to her husband that she wanted to quit, but he urged her to stick things out at least until the end of the semester. Today she admits how grateful she is for that advice. "Once I got used to things," she explains, "I started loving school. Ironically, I enjoyed my botany classes much more than I had enjoyed anthropology courses and found I did better in them." Soon she was awarded a fellowship to teach undergraduate courses in the biology department for the academic year 1979—80.

Now armed with special techniques both in botany and archaeology, Mary Dunn has far more professional skills than most people but still cannot find permanent employment as a college professor or regular employment as a free-lance archaeologist. "The biggest problem I have," she admits, "is that I am not free to do much work that will take me away from the family for very long periods."

But does she regret all the time and effort she has invested in becoming a professional archaeologist? Hardly. As she explains, "I went through the whole process of turning to other fields and coming around full circle to realize that I am an anthropologist because I love my work. As a result of that revelation, I have discovered that I can be active in my field and make contributions in a number of other ways. I do not have to worry about supporting my family, so I have the opportunity to pursue other avenues, which include writing, museum research, library research, lectures, professional societies, volunteer programs for school children, and generally working in a way that my knowledge and expertise may be educational to others and contribute to my profession. I am not nearly as limited as I would be in a set academic environment. I am free to be as creative as I like and to work at my own pace."

Dr. Dunn collecting plants at site of Indian mound in Louisiana, 1978, for archaeobotanical reference collection *Photo by L. Lawrence Beavers*

GLOSSARY

adobe—brick made of sun-dried clay, sometimes containing straw
alluvial fan—a fan-shaped silt deposit of a stream where it issues from a gorge upon a plain or of a tributary stream at its junction with the main stream
Amazonian—pertaining to the Amazon River in South America
anthropology—the study of humankind in terms of culture, language, and biology
archaeology—the scientific study of any group of people in past ages by excavation and description of their material remains (artifacts, fossils, etc.) and environment
archaic—related to an earlier or more primitive time
arroyo—a watercourse in an arid region, usually dry except after heavy rains
artifact—an object made or modified by human effort
backhoe—a piece of heavy dirt-moving equipment with a bulldozer in the front and an arm and claw in the back
Chaco—a tribe of prehistoric pueblo Indians that once resided in what is now northern New Mexico
classical archaeology—archaeology relating to the cultures of the ancient Greeks and Romans
classics—ancient Greek and Roman works of literature and art
cultural resources management—a branch of archaeology relating to government preservation of our historic and prehistoric heritage
culture—the characteristic ways of living of a particular group of people at a particular time
curator—a person in charge of a museum or place of exhibition

dig—an archaeological excavation site, or the excavation itself

dissertation—an extended research paper, especially the one required before a candidate earns the Ph.D. (doctor of philosophy) degree

epigraphy—the study and deciphering of inscriptions

ethnology—the branch of anthropology that compares and analyzes cultures; sometimes known as cultural anthropology

excavation—the process of digging and cutting into the earth and exposing the site's strata and artifacts

Etruscan—pertaining to the pre-Roman civilization of Etruria in central Italy

fauna—the animal life of a given region or period of time

field schools—outdoor schools, usually operating in the summer and sometimes offering college or high school credit, which train students in archaeological or other special techniques

field work—scientific investigation or other work conducted outdoors, or away from the classroom

fossil—the remains of ancient plant or animal life that have been preserved in rock

geology—the study of the earth, its rocks, and its changes since the beginning of time

glyph—a picture or symbol carved in stone as an ancient form of writing

historic—relating to past events that occurred after the development of written language

in situ—in the original or natural position

linguistics—the study of language

loam—a loose soil composed of clay and sand that usually contains organic matter, which makes the soil very fertile

Makah—a tribe of whale-hunting Indians residing in the northwestern United States and in Canada

mammoth—a large, extinct species of elephant with hairy coat and long, curved tusks

manioc—Spanish word for cassava; any of several tropical plants that are cultivated for their edible, tuberous roots

mastodon—a large, extinct mammal resembling the mammoth and elephant but differing from them in the shape of its molars

Maya—an Indian people of Yucatán, British Honduras, northern Guatemala, and Mexico whose languages are Mayan

Mesoamerica—a geographic area that includes most of Mexico as well as the central American countries of Guatemala, Belize, El Salvador, Honduras, Nicaragua, Costa Rica, and Panama

New World archaeology—archaeology of the Western Hemisphere (North America, Mesoamerica, South America)

organic—matter that was once alive; derived from plants or animals

paleo—a prefix relating to ancient forms or conditions

paleolithic—pertaining to the second period of the Stone Age; characterized by rough or chipped stone tools
paleontology—the science of studying past life from fossil remains
petroglyph—a prehistoric drawing or carving on rock
physical anthropology—the study of human evolution and the present races of mankind
postceramic—after the period when the people of a given culture learned to make pottery
postdoctoral—relating to the training or career of a person who has already earned a doctor's degree
potsherd—a fragment of pottery
pre-Columbian—prior to 1492, the year of Columbus's discovery of the New World
predoctoral—relating to academic work done before a person has earned a doctor's degree
prehistory—events that occurred before the existence of written records
projectile point—an arrowhead or other sharp object propelled through the air
ranchero—a person who owns or works on a ranch, especially in Latin America or the southwestern United States
salvage archaeology—excavations that are designed to permit study of data from sites scheduled to be destroyed for construction of dams, highways, buildings, etc., and are usually undertaken under a contract specifying completion by a certain date
screens—wire mesh through which archaeologists painstakingly sift the dirt they have excavated in order to recover small artifacts
sediment—matter that settles to the bottom of water or other liquid
shards, sherds—*see* potsherds
silt—fine-grained soil and sand deposited by water
site—the area containing the remains of a past culture
sloth—a sluggish mammal that inhabits tropical forests and feeds on leaves and fruit
specimen—a part representing the whole or a single item representing many
strata—layers of soil and rock distinguishable by color, texture, etc.
stratigraphy—the arrangement of strata
tapir—a stout-bodied, hoofed mammal, somewhat resembling the swine
thesis—a long research paper, especially the paper required before a candidate earns a master's degree
Yaqui—an Indian tribe, of Sonora, Mexico, that takes its name from the river on which the Indians formerly lived
Zapotec—a Mexican tribe of agricultural Indians that lived in S. Oaxaca and on the Isthmus of Tehuantepec at the time of the Spanish invasion

APPENDIX 1

ARCHAEOLOGICAL FIELD SCHOOLS

Alabama

University of Alabama

Fees: R—$330; NR—$703; cooperative dormitory
Prerequisites: none
Address: Registrar; U Alabama; University, AL 35401; or Joseph O. Vogal; Dept of Anth; U Alabama; Box 6135; University, AL 35401

Arizona

Arizona State University

Fees: $29/credit; room and board $500
Prerequisites: none
Address: R. Christopher Goodwin; Dept of Anth; Arizona State U; Tempe, AZ 85281

University of Arizona

Fees: $240; food $200
Prerequisites: upper level undergrads; 3.0 GPA
Address: J. Jefferson Reid; Director, Arch Field School; Dept of Anth; U Arizona; Tucson, AZ 85721

Northern Arizona University

Fees: $550, includes room and board
Prerequisites: anthropology major or previous course in archaeology
Address: J. Richard Ambler; Dept of Anth; Box 15200; Northern Arizona U; Flagstaff, AZ 86011

Arkansas

University of Arkansas

Fees: R—$138; NR—$327; room and board extra
Prerequisites: senior or grad
Address: CRM Institute Coordinator; U Arkansas Museum; Fayetteville, AR 72701

California

California Polytechnic State University

Fees: $357; cooperative housekeeping
Prerequisites: high school grad
Address: Robert L. Hoover, Actg Chair; Dept of Social Sciences; California Poly State U; San Luis Obispo, CA 93407

California State University

Fees: $117; room and board extra
Prerequisites: none
Address: E. Jane Rosenthal; Dept of Anth; California State U; Long Beach, CA 90840

Colorado

Colorado State University

Fees: R—$96; NR—$324; room and board extra
Address: Elizabeth A. Morris; Dept of Anth; Colorado State U; Ft Collins, CO 80523

Colorado State University

Fees: R—$192; NR—$684; room and board extra
Address: Calvin Jennings; Dept of Anth; Colorado State U; Ft Collins, CO 80523

University of Denver

Fees: $495; room and board $150
Address: Sarah M. Nelson; Dept of Anth; U Denver; Denver CO 80210

Ft Lewis College

Fees: R—$123; NR—$410; room and board $196
Prerequisites: none for lower level course; field school for advanced course
Address: Admissions Office; Ft Lewis Coll; Durango, CO 81301

Connecticut

American Indian Archaeological Institute
Fees: $700, includes room and board
Prerequisites: none
Address: Russell G. Handsman; Research Dept; American Indian Arch Inst; Box 260; Washington, CT 06793

Central Connecticut State College
Fees: $257; room and board extra
Prerequisites: high school grad
Address: Frederic Warner; Dept of Anth; Central Connecticut State Coll; 1615 Stanley St; New Britain, CT 06050

Central Connecticut State College
Fees: $257; room and board extra
Prerequisites: none
Address: Kenneth L. Feder, Dept of Anth, Central Connecticut State Coll, 1615 Stanley St, New Britain, CT 06050

University of Connecticut
Fees: $45/credit; room and board extra
Prerequisites: none
Address: Jackie Bradley; Dept of Anth; Arch & Human Ecology; Box U-176; Storrs, CT 06268

District of Columbia

Catholic University
Fees: $460; room and board $60/wk
Prerequisites: undergrad or grad status
Address: William M. Gardner; Dept of Anth; Catholic U; Washington, DC 20064

Catholic University
Fees: vary, $150 up; room and board $60/wk
Prerequisites: high school status (this program is designed for students in grades 10—12)
Address: John J. Gilheany; Director, Summer Session; Catholic U; Washington, D.C. 20064

Catholic University
Fees: $540; includes camp facilities and food
Prerequisites: high school grad
Address: Errett Callahan; Pamunkey Research Ctr; Rt 1; Box 217 AA; Pamunkey Indian Reservation; King William, VA 23086

Florida

Florida State University

Fees: $198– $648; room and board $100
Prerequisites: junior, major in anthropology
Address: Kathleen Deagan; G-24 Bellamy; Florida State U; Tallahassee, FL 32306

University of South Florida

Fees: R–$158; NR–$683; insurance, $25
Prerequisites: undergrad
Address: J. Raymond Williams; Dept of Anth; U South Florida; Tampa FL 33620

Georgia

Georgia State University

Fees: R–$120; NR–$370; $22/wk for meals
Prerequisites: permission of director
Address: Roy S. Dickson, Jr.; Dept of Anth; Georgia State U; Atlanta, GA 30303

Hawaii

University of Hawaii

Fees: $30/credit; $5 fee
Prerequisites: introductory anthropology
Address: P. Bion Griffin; Dept of Anth; U Hawaii; Honolulu, HI 96822

Idaho

Idaho State University

Fees: R–$120; NR–$145; room, board, and supplies $400
Prerequisites: 3.0 GPA; introductory course in archaeology
Address: Mark Druss; Dept of Soc/Anth/Soc Wk; Campus Box 8215; Idaho State U; Pocatello, ID 83209

Illinois

University of Illinois

Fees: R–$180; NR–$480; room and board extra
Prerequisites: introductory anthropology
Address: Robert L. Hall; Director, Field School in Arch; Dept of Anth; U Illinois; Chicago Circle; Box 4348; Chicago, IL 60680

University of Illinois
Fees: $147—$462; $100 for field expenses; $18 insurance
Prerequisites: introductory anthropology or permission of instructor
Address: Charles J. Bareis; Dept of Anth; 109 Davenport Hall; U Illinois, Urbana, IL 61801

Northwestern University
Fees: grad—$600; undergrad—$420; room, board, and health $360
Prerequisites: none
Address: Paul J. Shanks; Field School Coordinator; Dept of Anth; Northwestern U; 2000 Sheridan Rd; Evanston, IL 60201

Southern Illinois University
Fees: $215–$480
Address: Jon D. Miller; Field School in Arch; Ctr for Arch Investigations; Southern Illinois U; Carbondale, IL 62901

Indiana

Ball State University
Fees: undergrad—$172; grad—$188; application fee $10
Prerequisites: undergrad and grad
Address: B. K. Swartz; Dept of Anth; Ball State U; Muncie, IN 47306

Ball State University
Fees: undergrad—$172; grad—$188; application fee $10
Prerequisites: undergrad and grad
Address: Ronald Hicks; Dept of Anth; Ball State U; Muncie, IN 47306

Iowa

Iowa State University
Fees: $243–$523; room and board extra
Prerequisites: introductory archaeology or permission of instructor
Address: David M. Gradwohl; Dept of Soc/Anth; 103 East Hall; Iowa State U; Ames IA 50011

University of Iowa
Fees: $108; room and board $207
Prerequisites: none
Address: John H. Haefner; Dept of Education; N106 East Hall; U Iowa; Iowa City, IA 52242

University of Iowa
Fees: $128–$432
Prerequisites: none
Address: Duane Anderson; State Archaeologist; 3 Jefferson Bldg; U Iowa; Iowa City, IA 52242

Kansas

Kansas State Historical Society
Prerequisites: membership in the Kansas Anthropological Association
Address: Kansas Anthropological Association, Kansas State Historical Society; 120 West 10th; Topeka, KS 66612

Wichita State University
Fees: R—$17/credit; NR—$50/credit; students receive minimum wage; room and board extra
Prerequisites: introductory anthropology; two letters of recommendation
Address: Donald Blakeslee; Dept of Anth; Wichita State U; Wichita, KS 67208

Kentucky

Northern Kentucky University
Fees: R—$20/credit; NR—$53/credit; room and board extra
Prerequisites: field methods
Address: James F. Hopgood; Dept of Anth; Northern Kentucky U; Highland Hts, KY 41076

Louisiana

Northern Louisiana University
Fees: R—$70; NR—$175; special fee $50; room and board $240
Prerequisites: none
Address: Glen S. Greene; Dept of Geosciences; Northeast Louisiana U; Monroe, LA 71201

Maine

University of Maine/University of Alberta

Fees: $38/credit–$100/credit; room and board extra
Prerequisites: grad or advanced undergrad
Address: David Young; Dept of Anth; U Alberta; Edmonton, AB T6G 2E2

University of Southern Maine

Fees: $270; students provide camping gear
Prerequisites: introductory arch
Address: David R. Yesner; Dept of Geog/Anth; U Southern Maine; Gorham, ME 04038

Maryland

University of Maryland

Fees: $38/credit–$100/credit; room and board extra
Prerequisites: permission of instructor
Address: Field School Director; Dept of Anth; Machmer Hall; U Massachusetts; Amherst, MA 01003

Massachusetts

Harvard University

Fees: $750; room, board, and equipment $690
Prerequisites: students must be sixteen years old and have completed eleventh grade
Address: Russell J. Barber; Peabody Museum; Harvard U; 11 Divinity Av; Cambridge, MA 02138

University of Massachusetts

Fees: undergrad $180; grad $240; fees $67
Prerequisites: major in anth
Address: Field School Director; Dept of Anth; Machmer Hall; U Massachusetts; Amherst, MA 01003

Old Sturbridge Village

Fees: $275; room and board $480
Prerequisites: soph standing
Address: John Worrell; Staff Archaeologist; Field School Director; Old Sturbridge Village; Sturbridge, MA 01566

Michigan

Central Michigan University
- Fees: $250, includes insurance
- Prerequisites: some archaeology preferred
- Address: Fel V. Brunett; Saginaw Archaeological Commission; 500 Federal Av; Box 359; Saginaw, MI 48606

Michigan State University
- Fees: R—$25/credit; NR—$52/credit; housing provided
- Prerequisites: none
- Address: William A. Lovis; Curator; Michigan State U Museum; East Lansing, MI 48824

Michigan Technological University
- Fees: field school $216; lab course $72
- Prerequisites: introductory archaeology
- Address: Patrick E. Martin; Dept of Soc Sci; Michigan Tech U; Houghton, MI 49931

Western Michigan University
- Fees: $159–$467
- Prerequisites: permission of instructor
- Address: William M. Cremin; Dept of Anth; Western Michigan U; Kalamazoo, MI 49008

Minnesota

Hamline University
- Fees: $255; room and board extra
- Prerequisites: introductory field methods; high school students accepted
- Address: Christy A. H. Caine; Director; Arch Program; Hamline U; St. Paul, MN 55104

University of Minnesota
- Fees: $17/credit
- Prerequisites: introductory anthropology
- Address: Guy Gibbon; Director; Summer Field School; Dept of Anth; 215 Ford Hall; U Minnesota; Minneapolis, MN 55455

Montana

Eastern Montana College

Fees: $25–$75

Prerequisites: previous classwork preferred

Address: C. Adrian Heidenreich; Native American Studies Program; Eastern Montana Coll; Billings, MT 59101

Anthro Research, Inc.

Fees: $60/day includes equipment and meals

Prerequisites: none

Address: Larry A. Lahren; Box 1218; Livingston, MT 59047

Nebraska

University of Nebraska

Fees: $203–$549; includes transportation and housing

Prerequisites: introductory anthropology

Address: Dale R. Henning; Dept of Anth; U Nebraska; Lincoln, NE 68588

Nevada

University of Nevada

Fees: $150; room and board $150

Prerequisites: introductory course in anthropology or archaeology or permission of instructor

Address: Margaret M. Lyneis; Director; Arch Field School; Dept of Anth; U Nevada; Las Vegas, NV 89154

University of Nevada

Fees: $250

Prerequisites: some background in North American archaeology desirable

Address: David Hurst Thomas; Chair, Dept of Anth; American Museum of Natural History; Central Park West at 79th St; New York, NY 10024

New Jersey

Monmouth College

Fees: undergrad $95/credit; grad $100/credit; lab fee $15

Prerequisites: cultural anthropology, introductory archaeology

Address: John A. Cavallo; Arch Research Lab; Monmouth Coll; West Long Branch, NJ 07764

New Mexico

Archaeological Society of New Mexico
Fees: $25/wk
Prerequisites: none
Address: Harry L. Hadlock; Box 397; Fruitland, NM 87416

New Mexico Highlands University
Fees: $125–$395
Prerequisites: introductory anthropology
Address: Robert Mishler, Arch Field Director; Dept of Behav Sci; New Mexico Highlands U; Las Vegas, NM 87701

University of New Mexico
Fees: $144–$440
Prerequisites: high school grad
Address: Linda S. Cordell; Summer Field School; Dept of Anth; U New Mexico; Albuquerque, NM 87131

New York

Buffalo State College
Fees: $160; room and board extra
Prerequisites: none
Address: Bill Engelbrecht; Dept of Anth; Buffalo State Coll; 1300 Elmwood Av; Buffalo, NY 14222

Hebrew Union College
Location: Israel
Fees: $1,125, includes travel, room, and board
Prerequisites: none
Address: Paul M. Steinberg; Dan Volunteer Program; 40 West 68th St; New York, NY 10023

New York University
Fees: $500; room and board about $200
Prerequisites: at least one anthropology course
Address: Burt Salwen; Dept of Anth; New York U; 25 Waverly Pl; New York, NY 10003

State University of New York College
Fees: $25/credit and up; room $24–$36/wk; board $20/wk
Prerequisites: permission of instructor
Address: Robert C. Davidson; Director, Summer Session; SUNY Coll; New Paltz, NY 12562

State University of New York College
Fees: $25/credit and up
Prerequisites: permission of instructor
Address: William A. Starna; Dept of Anth; SUNY Coll; Oneonta, NY 13820

State University of New York College
Location: Guatemala
Fees: $242; room and board $150; airfare $550; incidentals $150
Prerequisites: permission of instructor
Address: Steven J. Marqusee; Dept of Anth; SUNY Coll; Potsdam, NY 13676

State University of New York
Fees: R—$270; NR—$450; room and board extra
Prerequisites: permission of instructor
Address: Dean R. Snow; Chair, Dept of Anth; SUNY; Albany, NY 12222

State University of New York
Fees: $271 and up
Prerequisites: anthropology major
Address: Office of Summer Sessions; SUNY; Binghamton, NY 13901

State University of New York
Address: Ezra Zubrow; Dept of Anth; 581-L; Building 5; Spaulding Quad; SUNY; Buffalo, NY 14261

Rensselaer Polytechnic Institute
Fees: $840
Prerequisites: previous course work
Address: Sherene Baugher-Perlin; Rensselaer Polytech Inst, Dept of Anth/Soc; Troy, NY 12181

Rochester Museum & Science Center
Fees: $35
Prerequisites: none
Address: Robert Sullivan; Rochester Museum & Science Ctr; 657 East Av; PO Box 1480; Rochester, NY 14603

North Carolina

Western Carolina University

Fees: R—$140; NR—$302; board $22/wk

Prerequisites: permission of director

Address: Roy S. Dickens, Jr.; Dept of Anth; Georgia State U; Atlanta, GA 30303

Ohio

University of Cincinnati

Fees: $216–$648

Prerequisites: permission of director

Address: Kent D. Vickery; Director, Field Course in Arch; Dept of Anth; U Cincinnati; Cincinnati, OH 45221

Cleveland State University

Fees: R—$280; NR—$416; room and board $392

Prerequisites: normal academic progress

Address: John Lallo; Director, Field School; Dept of Anth; Cleveland State U; 1983 East 24th St; Cleveland, OH 44115

Cuyahoga Community College

Fees: Cuyahoga R—$60; Ohio R—$84; NR—$144

Prerequisites: none

Address: Daniel A. Grossman; Head; Dept of Behav Sciences; Western Campus; Cuyahoga Community Coll; 11000 Pleasant Valley Rd; Parma, OH 44130

Defiance College

Fees: $377

Prerequisites: none

Address: Robert Boehm; Dept of Hist; Defiance Coll; Defiance, OH 43512

Ohio University

Fees: R—$352; NR—$800

Prerequisites: introductory anthropology

Address: Barbara Thiel; Dept of Soc/Anth; Carnegie Hall; Athens, OH 45701

Wright State University

Fees: $290 and up; room and board extra

Prerequisites: none

Address: Robert V. Riordan; Director; Dept of Soc/Anth; Wright State U; Dayton, OH 45435

Oklahoma

Oklahoma State University
Fees: $450; includes room and board
Address: Annetta L. Cheek; 301 Dairy Bldg; Oklahoma State U; Stillwater, OK 74074

University of Oklahoma
Fees: $18/credit and up
Prerequisites: none
Address: Susan C. Vehik; Dept of Anth; S21 Dale Hall Tower; U Oklahoma; Norman, OK 73069

Oregon

Oregon State University
Fees: undergrad $230; grad $340
Address: David Brauner, or Richard E. Ross; Dept of Anth; Oregon State U; Corvallis, OR 97330

University of Oregon
Fees: undergrad $265; grad $410; transportation $50
Address: Rick Minor; Dept of Anth; U Oregon; Eugene, OR 97403

University of Oregon
Fees: undergrad $265; grad $410; subsistence $150
Address: C. Melvin Aikens; Dept of Anth; U Oregon; Eugene, OR 97403

Pennsylvania

Clarion State College
Fees: R—$39/credit; NR—$71/credit; $10 fee; room and board $26.50/wk
Prerequisites: completion of grade 10 or 11
Address: Gustav A. Konitzky; Project Director, Student Science Training Program; Field Arch; Arch Lab; Clarion State Coll; Clarion, PA 16214

Clarion State College
Fees: R—$39/credit; NR—$71/credit; $10 fee; room and board $26.50/wk
Prerequisites: high school grad and college status
Address: Director, Field Programs; Arch Lab; Clarion State Coll; Clarion PA 16214

Gannon College
Fees: $75/credit; $10 fee; room and board $50/wk
Prerequisites: high school seniors or college students
Address: Director of Anth; Box 76; Gannon Coll; Erie, PA 16541

University of Pennsylvania
Fees: $455; room and board extra
Prerequisites: none
Address: Summer Sessions, U Pennsylvania; 210 Logan Hall; Philadelphia, PA 19174

University of Pittsburgh
Fees: $461–$1,261; board $20/wk
Prerequisites: firm background is welcome
Address: Joseph Yedlowski; Personnel Director, Summer Arch Field Program; Dept of Anth; U Pittsburgh; Pittsburgh, PA 15260

West Chester State College
Fees: R—$39/credit; NR—$71/credit
Prerequisites: none
Address: M. J. Becker; Dept of Anth; West Chester State Coll; West Chester, PA 19380

Rhode Island

Brown University
Fees: $631/session; room and board extra
Prerequisites: introductory archaeology recommended
Address: George H. Odell; Dept of Anth; Brown U; Providence RI 02912

Rhode Island College
Fees: R—$237; NR—$333
Prerequisites: course work or field experience
Address: E. Pierre Morenon; Dept of Anth/Geog; Gaige Hall; Rhode Island Coll; Providence, RI 02908

South Carolina

University of South Carolina
Fees: R—$30/credit; NR—$70/credit; $10 application fee
Prerequisites: permission of instructors
Address: Stanton W. Green; Dept of Anth; U South Carolina; Columbia, SC 29208

South Dakota

University of South Dakota

Fees: undergrad $23/credit; grad $31/credit; $150 lab fee; volunteers welcome

Prerequisites: none

Address: Darrell W. Fulmer; Mitchell Arch Site, Mitchell, SD 57301

Tennessee

University of Tennessee

Fees: $150–$472, includes room and board: $20 activities fee

Prerequisites: none

Address: Charles H. Faulkner; Dept of Anth; 249 South Stadium Hall; U Tennessee; Knoxville, TN 37916

Texas

Baylor University

Fees: $55/credit; volunteers welcome; room and breakfast provided

Prerequisites: sophomore standing

Address: James S. Belew; Box UB 113; Inst of Arch; Baylor U; Waco TX 76703

Southern Methodist University

Fees: $420; room and board $455

Prerequisites: none

Address: Director; Ft Burgwin Research Ctr; Southern Methodist U; Dallas, TX 75275

Texas Tech University

Fees: R—$63; lab and field fees $30; room and board $457

Prerequisites: permission of instructor

Address: William J. Mayer-Oakes; Dept of Anth; Texas Tech U; Lubbock, TX 79409

University of Texas

Fees: R—$76; NR—$151; $50 lab fee; room and board extra

Prerequisites: introductory anthropology and letter from anthropology instructor

Address: Michael S. Foster; Dept of Soc/Anth; U Texas; El Paso, TX 79968

University of Texas
Fees: R—$66; NR—$281; board about $75
Prerequisites: permission of instructor
Address: Thomas Hester; Ctr for Arch Research; U Texas; San Antonio, TX 78285

Utah

Brigham Young University
Fees: Mormons $210; others $315; transportation $45; campus room and board $300
Prerequisites: archaeological classwork or experience
Address: John L. Sorenson; Chair; Dept of Anth/Arch; Brigham Young University; Provo, UT 84602

University of Utah
Fees: $650
Prerequisites: preference to advanced undergrads and to grads
Address: James F. O'Connell; Arch Ctr; Dept of Anth; 117 Stewart Bldg; U Utah; Salt Lake City, Utah 84112

Virginia

James Madison University
Fees: $16/credit and up
Prerequisites: none
Address: Clarence R. Geier; Director, Arch Field Program; Dept of Soc/Anth/Soc Wk; James Madison U; Harrisonburg, VA 22807

College of William and Mary
Fees: $670 includes room and board
Prerequisites: none for beginning course
Address: Theodore R. Reinhart; Director, Summer Field School; Dept of Anth; Coll of William and Mary; Williamsburg, VA 23185

Washington

Washington State University
Fees: $216 minimum
Prerequisites: admission by special application
Address: Dept of Anth; Washington U; Pullman, WA 99164

Washington State University
Fees: undergrad $216; grad $108
Prerequisites: two letters of recommendation
Address: Dale R. Croes; Director, Hoko River Arch Project; Dept of Anth; Washington State U; Pullman, WA 99164

Washington State University
Fees: $375
Address: J. Jeffrey Flenniken; Lithic Lab, Lab of Anth; Washington State U; Pullman, WA 99164

University of Washington
Fees: $229
Address: Garland Grabert; Dept of Anth; DH-05; U Washington; Seattle, WA 98195

University of Washington
Fees: $229; partial board $175
Prerequisites: none
Address: Donald K. Grayson; Dept of Anth; DH-05; U Washington; Seattle, WA 98195

West Virginia

Marshall University
Fees: R—$131; NR—$606; room and board extra
Prerequisites: introductory cultural anth, arch, or permission
Address: Office of Admissions; Marshall U; Huntington, WV 25701

Wisconsin

University of Wisconsin
Fees: $180–$1,308
Address: Lynne Goldstein; Dept of Anth; U Wisconsin; Milwaukee, WI 53201

University of Wisconsin
Fees: $231; room and board extra
Prerequisites: introductory archaeology
Address: Victoria Dirst; Dept of Soc/Anth; U Wisconsin; Oshkosh, WI 54901

Canada

University of Alberta

Fees: $195; room and board $135

Prerequisites: previous coursework desirable

Address: T. C. Losey; Director, Arch Field School; Dept of Anth; U Alberta; Edmonton, AB T6G 2H4

University of Manitoba

Fees: CDN $125; tents and some food provided

Prerequisites: permission of instructor

Address: G. Monks; Dept of Anth; U Manitoba; Winnipeg, MB R3T 2N2

Trent University

Location: Belize

Fees: $170 (write for estimates of travel and living expenses)

Prerequisites: previous background desirable

Address: Paul F. Healy, Actg Chair; Dept of Anth; Trent U; Peterborough, ON K9J 7B8

NOTE: Of particular interest to high school students and lay adults is EARTHWATCH, a nonprofit organization that conducts scientific expeditions involving various subjects, including archaeology. For a free catalog, send to the address below:

EARTHWATCH
10 Juniper Road
Box 127M
Belmont, Massachusetts 02178

APPENDIX 2

DEPARTMENTS OF ANTHROPOLOGY/ ARCHAEOLOGY

(For information about exact degrees offered by each institution, write for catalogs at the addresses listed.)

Adelphi University
Admissions, Levermore Hall, Adelphi U, Garden City, NY 11530
University of Alabama, Birmingham
Admissions, U of Alabama, University Sta, Birmingham, AL 35294
University of Alabama, University
Admissions and Records, 152 Rose Administration Bldg, U of Alabama, University, AL 35486
University of Alaska, Anchorage
Registrar, 2651 Providence Dr, Anchorage AK 99504
University of Alaska, Fairbanks
Registrar, Box 95162, U of Alaska, Fairbanks, AK 99701
University of Alberta
Faculty of Grad Studies, U of Alberta, Edmonton, AB T6G OX7, Canada
American University
Office of Admissions, The American University, Washington, D.C. 20016
Amherst College
Admissions, Amherst College, Amherst, MA 01002
Appalachian State University
Admissions, Appalachian State U, Boone, NC 28608
Arizona State University
Dean, Grad College, Arizona State U, Tempe, AZ 85281

University of Arizona
　Dean, Grad Coll, or Undergrad Advisor, U of Arizona, Tucson, AZ 85721
University of Arkansas
　Graduate Coordinator, Dept of Anth, U of Arkansas, Fayetteville, AR 72701
Ball State University
　Chmn, Dept of Anth, Ball State U, Muncie, IN 47306
Bard College
　Admissions, Bard Coll, Annandale-on-Hudson, NY 12504
Barnard College
　Admissions, Barnard Coll, 606 W 120 St., New York, NY 10027
Baylor University
　Admissions, Pat Neff Hall, Baylor University, Waco, TX 76703
Beloit College
　Admissions, Beloit College, Beloit, WI 53511
Bethel College
　Registrar, Bethel College, 3900 Bethel Drive, St Paul, MN 55112
Bloomsburg State College
　Admissions, Bloomsburg State C, Bloomsburg, PA 17815
Boise State University
　Admissions, Boise State U, 1910 University Dr, Boise, ID 83725
Boston University
　Admissions, Boston U, 121 Bay State Rd, Boston, MA 02215
Bowdoin College
　Admissions, Bowdoin Coll, Brunswick, ME 04011
Brandeis University
　Admissions, Brandeis U, Waltham, MA 02154
Brigham Young University
　Mailing/Answering Service, Brigham Young U, Provo, UT 84602
Brock University
　Registrar, Brock U, St Catharines, ON L2S 3A1, Canada
Brooklyn College
　Registrar, Brooklyn Coll, CUNY, Bedford Av & Av H, Brooklyn, NY 11210
Brown University
　Admissions, Brown U, Providence, RI 02912
Bryn Mawr College
　Admissions, Bryn Mawr Coll, Bryn Mawr, PA 19010
University of Calgary
　Registrar, U of Calgary, Calgary, AB T2N 1N4, Canada

California State College, San Bernardino
Admissions and Records, California State Coll, San Bernardino, CA 92407
California State College, Stanislaus
Registrar, California State Coll, Stanislaus, 800 Monte Vista, Turlock, CA 95380
California State University, Chico
Registrar, California State U, Chico, CA 95929
California State University, Dominguez Hills
Admissions, California State U, Dominguez Hills, Carson, CA 90747
California State University, Fresno
Dept of Anth, California State U, Fresno, CA 93740
California State University, Fullerton
Dean, Grad Studies, 801 Langsdorf Hall, California State U, Fullerton, CA 92634
California State University, Hayward
Campus Bookstore, California State U, Hayward, CA 94542
California State University, Long Beach
Dean, Grad Studies, California State U, 1250 Bellflower Blvd, Long Beach, CA 90840
California State University, Los Angeles
Admissions, California State U, Los Angeles, CA 90032
California State University, Northridge
Grad Studies Office, California State U, 18111 Nordhoff St, Northridge, CA 91324
California State University, Sacramento
Admissions, California State U, 6000 Jay St, Sacramento, CA 95819
University of California, Berkeley
Admissions and Records, Sproul Hall, U of California, Berkeley, CA 94720
University of California, Davis
Registrar, U of California, Davis, CA 95616
University of California, Irvine
Viviane Wayne, U of California, Irvine, CA 92717
University of California, Los Angeles
Registrar, U of California, Los Angeles, CA 90024
University of California, Riverside
Registrar, U of California, Riverside CA 92521
University of California, San Diego
Registrar, U of California, San Diego, La Jolla, CA 92037
University of California, San Francisco
Registrar, U of California, San Francisco, CA 94143

University of California, Santa Barbara
Grad Adviser, Dept of Anth, U of California, Santa Barbara, CA 93106
University of California, Santa Cruz
Enrollment, U of California, Santa Cruz, CA 95064
Carleton College
Admissions, Carleton Coll, Northfield, MN 55057
Case Western Reserve University
Dean, Grad Sch, Case Western Reserve U, Cleveland, OH 44106
Catholic University of America
Registrar, Catholic U of America, Washington, DC 20064
Central Connecticut State College
Admissions, Central Connecticut State C, New Britain, CT 06050
The University of Central Florida
Dept of Sociology, University of Central Florida, Orlando FL 32618
Central Michigan University
Registrar, Central Michigan U, Mt Pleasant, MI 48859
Central Washington University
Admissions, Central Washington U, Ellensburg, WA 98926
University of Chicago
Dean of Students, Div of Soc Scis, 1130 E. 59th St, Chicago, IL 60637
University of Cincinnati
Dept of Anth, 1118 Crosley Tower, U of Cincinnati, OH 45221
City College of the City University of New York
Registrar, City C, CUNY, Convent Av and W 138th St, New York, NY 10031
City University of New York
Registrar, City U Ctr, 33 W 42nd St, New York, NY 10036
Cleveland State University
Admissions, Cleveland State U, Cleveland, OH 44115
Colgate University
Admissions, Colgate U, Hamilton, NY 13346
Colorado College
Admissions, Colorado Coll, Colorado Springs, CO 80903
Colorado State University
Admissions, Colorado State U, Fort Collins, CO 80523
University of Colorado, Boulder
Admissions & Records (enclose $2), Regent Hall 125, U of Colorado, Boulder, CO 80309
University of Colorado, Denver
Bookstore (enclose $1.25), 1100 14th St, U of Colorado, Denver, CO 80202

Columbia University
Admissions, Columbia U, New York, NY 10027
Teachers College, Columbia University
Admissions, Box 302, Columbia U, 525 W 120th St, New York, NY 10027
Connecticut College
Admissions, Connecticut Coll, New London, CT 06320
University of Connecticut
Grad Admissions, Box U-6A, U of Connecticut, Storrs, CT 06268
Cornell University
Grad Sch, Sage Grad Ctr, Cornell U, Ithaca, NY 14853
Dalhousie University
Registrar, Dalhousie U, Halifax, NS, Canada
Dartmouth College
Admissions, Dartmouth C, Hanover, NH 03755
University of Delaware
Admissions & Records, U of Delaware, Newark, DE 19711
University of Denver
Admissions & Records, U of Denver, Denver, CO 80208
Drew University
Registrar, Drew U, Madison, NJ 07940
Duke University
Admissions, Duke U, Durham, NC 27706
East Carolina University
Registrar, East Carolina U, Greenville, NC 27834
Eastern Kentucky University
Admissions, E Kentucky U, Richmond, KY 40475
Eastern New Mexico University
Dean Grad Sch, E New Mexico U, Portales, NM 88130
Emory University
Admissions, Emory U, Atlanta, GA 30322
Florida Atlantic University
Admissions, Florida Atlantic U, Boca Raton, FL 33431
Florida International University
Admissions, Florida International University, Tamiami Trail, Miami, FL 33199
Florida State University
Registrar, Florida State U, Tallahassee, FL 32306
University of Florida
Admissions, 135 Tigert Hall, U of Florida, Gainesville, FL 32611
Fordham University
Admissions, Fordham U, Bronx, NY 10458

Fort Lewis College
Admissions, Ft Lewis Coll, Durango, CO 81301
Franklin and Marshall College
Admissions, Franklin & Marshall Coll, Lancaster, PA 17604
George Mason University
Admissions, George Mason U, Fairfax, VA 22030
George Washington University
Admissions, George Washington U, Washington, DC 20052
Georgia State University
Registrar, Georgia State U, Atlanta, GA 30303
University of Georgia
Registrar, U of Georgia, Athens, GA 30602
Grinnell College
Registrar, Grinnell Coll, Grinnell, IA 50112
University of Guam
Admissions, Box EK, U of Guam, Agana, Guam 96910
Hamilton College
Registrar, Hamilton and Kirkland Colleges, Hamilton Coll, Clinton, NY 13323
University of Hartford
Addressing Services, U of Hartford, 200 Bloomfield Av, West Hartford, CT 06117
Hartwick College
Registrar, Hartwick Coll, Oneonta, NY 13820
Harvard University
Grad Sch of Arts & Scis, Byerly Hall, Harvard U, Cambridge, MA 02138
University of Hawaii, Honolulu
Office of Univ Relations, 2444 Dole St, U of Hawaii, Honolulu, HI 96822
Hobart and William Smith Colleges
Admissions, Hobart & Wm Smith Coll, Geneva, NY 14456
University of Houston
Registrar, U of Houston, Houston, TX 77002
Howard University
Admissions, Howard U, Washington, DC 20059
Hunter College of the City University of New York
Registrar, Hunter C, CUNY, 695 Park Av, New York, NY 10021
Idaho State University
Anth Program, Idaho State U, Box 8005, Pocatello, ID 83209
University of Idaho
Admissions, U of Idaho, Moscow, ID 83843

Illinois State University
Admissions, Illinois State U, Normal, IL 61761
University of Illinois, Chicago Circle
Grand Coll, U of Illinois, Chicago Cir, Chicago, IL 60680
University of Illinois, Urbana-Champaign
Admissions & Records, 10 Admin Bldg, U of Illinois, Urbana, IL 61801
Incarnate Word College
Admissions, Incarnate Word Coll, 4301 Broadway, San Antonio, TX 78209
Indiana State University
Registrar, Indiana State U, Terre Haute, IN 47809
Indiana University
Dean, Grad Sch, Indiana U, Bloomington, IN 47405
Iowa State University
Admissions, 105 Beardshear Hall, Iowa State U, Ames, IA 50010
University of Iowa
Dept of Anth, U of Iowa, Iowa City, IA 52242
Johns Hopkins University
Dept of Anth, Johns Hopkins U, Baltimore, MD 21218
Kansas State University
Admissions & Records, Kansas State U, Manhattan, KS 66506
University of Kansas
Dept of Anth, U of Kansas, Lawrence, KS 66045
Kent State University
Admissions, Kent State U, Kent, OH 44242
University of Kentucky
Admissions, U of Kentucky, Lexington, KY 40506
Kenyon College
Registrar, Kenyon Coll, Gambier, OH 43022
Kutztown State College
Admissions, Kutztown State Coll, Kutztown, PA 19530
Lafayette College
Admissions, Lafayette Coll, Easton, PA 18042
Lake Forest College
Dept of Soc & Anth, Lake Forest, IL 60045
Laurentian University
Registrar, Laurentian U, Sudbury, ON P3E 2C6, Canada
Laval University
Dept d'Anth, U Laval, Cite U, Quebec, 10 PQ GIK 7P4, Canada
Lawrence University
Admissions, Lawrence U, Appleton, WI 54911

Lehigh University
Dean, Grad Sch, Lehigh U, Bethlehem, PA 18015
Herbert H. Lehman College of the City University of New York
Registrar, Herbert H. Lehman Coll, CUNY, Bedford Pk & Blvd W, Bronx, NY 10467
University of Lethbridge
Registrar, U of Lethbridge, Lethbridge, AB T1K 3M4, Canada
Loma Linda University
Admissions, Loma Linda U, Riverside, CA 92515
Longwood College
Admissions, Longwood Coll, Farmville, VA 23901
Louisiana State University, Baton Rouge
Registrar, Louisiana State U, Baton Rouge, LA 70803
University of Louisville
Registrar, U of Louisville, Louisville, KY 40208
Loyola University of Chicago
Dean, Grad Sch, Loyola U, 6525 N Sheridan Rd, Chicago, IL 60626
Macalester College
Admissions, Macalester Coll, St Paul, MN 55105
University of Maine, Orono
Admissions, U of Maine, Orono, ME 04473
University of Manitoba
Registrar, U of Manitoba, Winnipeg, MB R3T 2N2, Canada
Marquette University
Admissions, Marquette U, Milwaukee, WI 53233
University of Maryland, College Park
Registrar, U of Maryland, College Pk, MD 20742
Massachusetts Institute of Technology
Registrar, MIT, Cambridge, MA 02139
University of Massachusetts, Amherst
Dept of Anth, Machmer Hall, U of Mass, Amherst, MA 01003
University of Massachusetts, Boston
Admissions, U of Massachusetts, Harbor Campus, Boston, MA 02125
McGill University
Dept of Anth, McGill U, Leacock Bldg, 855 Sherbrooke West, Montreal, PQ H3A 2T7, Canada
McMaster University
Dept of Anth, McMaster U, Hamilton, ON L8S 4L9, Canada
Memorial University of Newfoundland
Admissions, Memorial U of Newfoundland, St John's, NF A1C 5S7, Canada

Memphis State University
    Records, Memphis State U, Memphis, TN 38152
Miami University
    Grad Sch, Admin Bldg, Miami U, Oxford, OH 45056
University of Miami
    Admissions, Box 248025, U of Miami, Coral Gables, FL 33124
Michigan State University
    Dept of Anth, 354 Baker Hall, Michigan State U, East Lansing, MI 48824
University of Michigan, Ann Arbor
    Admissions, U of Michigan, Ann Arbor, MI 48109
University of Michigan, Dearborn
    University Relations, U of Michigan, 4901 Evergreen Rd, Dearborn, MI 48128
Middlebury College
    Admissions, Middlebury Coll, Middlebury, VT 05753
University of Minnesota, Duluth
    Admissions, U of Minnesota, Duluth, MN 55812
University of Minnesota, Minneapolis
    Admissions & Records, 240 Williamson Hall, U of Minnesota, Minneapolis, MN 55455
Mississippi State University
    Registrar, Mississippi State U, Mississippi State, MS 39762
University of Mississippi
    Registrar, U of Mississippi, University, MS 38677
University of Missouri, Columbia
    Admissions, 130 Jesse Hall, U of Missouri, Columbia, MO 65211
University of Missouri, Kansas City
    Anth Dept, 5232 Rockhill Road, Kansas City, MO 64110
University of Missouri, St Louis
    Admissions, U of Missouri, 8001 Natural Bridge Rd, St Louis, MO 63121
Monmouth College
    Admissions, Wilson Hall, Monmouth Coll, West Long Branch, NJ 07764
Montana State University
    Publication and News Service, Montana State U, Bozeman, MT 59717
University of Montana
    Registrar, U of Montana, Missoula, MT 59812
Montclair State College
    Admissions, Montclair State Coll, Upper Montclair, NJ 07043

University of Montreal
 Dept d'Anth, U de Montreal, CP 6128, Succursale 'A' Montreal, PQ H3C 3J7, Canada
Mount Holyoke College
 Admissions, Mount Holyoke Coll, South Hadley, MA 01075
University of Nebraska
 Admissions, Grad Coll, Admin 412, U of Nebraska, Lincoln, NE 68588
University of Nevada, Las Vegas
 Admissions, U of Nevada, Las Vegas, NV 89154
University of Nevada, Reno
 Registrar, U of Nevada, Reno, NV 89557
University of New Brunswick
 Grad Sch, Arts & Education, Old Arts Bldg, U of New Brunswick, Fredericton, New Brunswick, Canada E3B 5A3
University of New Hampshire
 Admissions, U of New Hampshire, Durham, NH 03824
New Mexico Highlands University
 Behavioral Sciences, New Mexico Highlands U, Las Vegas, NM 87701
New Mexico State University
 Admissions, New Mexico State U, Las Cruces, NM 88003
University of New Mexico
 Bookstore, U of New Mexico, Albuquerque, NM 87131
University of New Orleans
 Registrar, U of New Orleans, New Orleans, LA 70122
New School for Social Research
 Admissions, New Sch for Social Research, 65 Fifth Av, New York, NY 10003
New York University
 Admissions, Anth, Tisch Hall, New York U, Washington Sq, 25 Waverly Pl, New York, NY 10003
State University of New York College, Brockport
 Registrar, SUNY C, Brockport, NY 14420
State University of New York College, Buffalo
 Dept of Anth, SUNY C, Buffalo, NY 14222
State University of New York College, Fredonia
 Admissions, Maytum Hall, SUNY C, Fredonia, NY 14063
State University of New York College, Geneseo
 Admissions, SUNY C, Geneseo, NY 14454
State University of New York College, New Paltz
 Admissions, SUNY C, New Paltz, NY 12561

State University of New York College, Oneonta
Admissions, SUNY C, Oneonta, NY 13820
State University of New York College, Oswego
Admissions, SUNY C, Oswego, NY 13126
State University of New York College, Plattsburgh
Registrar, SUNY C, Plattsburgh, NY 12901
State University of New York College, Potsdam
Admissions, SUNY C, Potsdam, NY 13676
State University of New York College, Purchase
Admissions, SUNY C, Purchase, NY 10577
State University of New York, Albany
Admissions, AD 214, SUNY, Albany, NY 12222
State University of New York, Binghamton
Admissions, SUNY, Binghamton, NY 13901
State University of New York, Buffalo
Admissions & Records, SUNY, Buffalo, NY 14261
State University of New York, Stony Brook
Director, Grad Studies, SUNY, Stony Brook, NY 11794
University of North Carolina, Chapel Hill
Admissions, U of North Carolina, Chapel Hill, NC 27514
University of North Carolina, Charlotte
Admissions, U of North Carolina, UNCC Station, Charlotte, NC 28223
University of North Carolina, Greensboro
Admissions, U of North Carolina, Greensboro, NC 27412
North Central College
Admissions, North Central Coll, Naperville, IL 60540
University of North Dakota
Dept of Anth, U of North Dakota, Grand Forks, ND 58201
Northeastern University
Grad Sch of Arts and Sciences, Northeastern U, Boston, MA 02115
Northeastern Illinois University
Information Desk, Northeastern Ill U, St Louis at Bryn Mawr Av, Chicago, IL 60625
Northern Arizona University
Registrar, Northern Arizona U, Flagstaff, AZ 86011
University of Northern Colorado
Public Affairs, U of Northern Colorado, Greeley, CO 80639
Northern Illinois University
Admissions, Northern Illinois U, DeKalb, IL 60115
University of Northern Iowa
Registrar, U of Northern Iowa, Cedar Falls, IA 50613

Northern Kentucky University
 Admissions, Northern Kentucky U, Highland Heights, KY 41076
Northwestern University
 Admissions, Northwestern U, Evanston, IL 60201
University of Notre Dame
 Admissions, U of Notre Dame, Notre Dame, IN 46556
Oakland University
 Admissions, Oakland U, Rochester, MI 48063
Oberlin College
 Admissions, Oberlin Coll, Oberlin, OH 44074
Occidental College
 Admissions, Occidental Coll, Los Angeles, CA 90041
Ohio State University
 Grad Sch, 230 N Oval Mall, Ohio State U, Columbus OH 43210
Ohio Wesleyan University
 Admissions, Ohio Wesleyan U, Delaware, OH 43015
Ohio University
 Ohio U Bulletin, Athens, OH 45701
University of Oklahoma
 Admissions & Records, U of Oklahoma, Norman, OK 73019
Oregon State University
 Registrar, Oregon State U, Corvallis, OR 97331
University of Oregon
 Publications, Box 3449, University St, U of Oregon, Eugene, OR 97403
Pennsylvania State University
 Admissions, 201 Shields Bldg, Pennsylvania State U, University Pk, PA 16802
University of Pennsylvania
 Admissions, College Hall, U of Pennsylvania, Philadelphia, PA 19104
University of Pittsburgh
 Dept of Anth, U of Pittsburgh, Pittsburgh, PA 15260
Pitzer College
 Admissions, Pitzer Coll, Claremont, CA 91711
Pomona College
 Admissions, Sumner Hall, Pomona Coll, Claremont, CA 91711
Portland State University
 Admissions, Portland State U, PO Box 751, Portland, OR 97207
Princeton University
 Admissions, Princeton U, Princeton, NJ 08544
Providence College
 Admissions, Providence Coll, Providence, RI 02918

Purdue University
Anth Sect, Dept of Soc & Anth, Purdue U, Lafayette, IN 47907
Queens College of the City University of New York
Registrar, Queens C., CUNY, 65-30 Kissena Blvd, Flushing, NY 11367
University of Regina
Dept of Anth, U of Regina, Regina, SK S4S OA2, Canada
Rensselaer Polytechnic Institute
Admissions, Rensselaer Polytechnic Inst, Troy, NY 12181
Rhode Island College
Admissions, Rhode Island Coll, Mt Pleasant Av, Providence, RI 02908
University of Rhode Island
Admissions, U of Rhode Island, Kingston, RI 02881
Rice University
Registrar, Rice U, Houston, TX 77001
Ripon College
Admissions, Ripon Coll, Ripon, WI 54971
Rochester Institute of Technology, Eisenhower College Campus
Dept of Anth, Rochester Inst of Tech, Eisenhower Coll Campus, Seneca Falls, NY 13148
University of Rochester
Admin Bldg, U of Rochester, NY 14627
Rollins College
Registrar, Rollins Coll, Winter Park, FL 32789
Rutgers University—the State University of New Jersey
Admissions, Rutgers U, New Brunswick, NJ 08903
St John Fisher College
Admissions, St John Fisher College, Rochester, NY 14618
St John's University
Dept of Soc and Anth, St John's U, Jamaica, NY 11439
St Lawrence University
Admissions, St Lawrence U, Canton, NY 13617
Saint Mary's University
Registrar, St Mary's U, Halifax NS B3H 3C3, Canada
San Diego State University
Dept of Anth, San Diego State U, San Diego, CA 92182
University of San Diego
Admissions, U San Diego, San Diego, CA 92110
San Francisco State University
Dept of Anth, San Francisco State U, CA 94132
San Jose State University
Dept of Anth, San Jose State U, San Jose, CA 95192

University of Santa Clara
U of Santa Clara, Santa Clara, CA 95053
Sarah Lawrence College
Registrar, Sarah Lawrence Coll, Bronxville, NY 10708
University of Saskatchewan
Registrar, U of Saskatchewan, Saskatoon, SK, Canada
Seton Hall University
Admissions, Seton Hall U, South Orange, NJ 07079
Simon Fraser University
Registrar, Simon Fraser U, Burnaby 2 BC V5A 1S6, Canada
Skidmore College
Admissions Office, Skidmore College, Saratoga Springs, NY 12866
Smith College
Admissions, Smith Coll, Northampton, MA 01060
Sonoma State University
Admissions, Stevenson Hall, Sonoma State U, 1801 East Cotati Av, Rohnert Pk, CA 94928
University of South Carolina
Registrar, U of South Carolina, Columbia, SC 29208
University of South Dakota
Admissions, U South Dakota, Vermillion, SD 57059
University of South Florida
Registrar, U of South Florida, Tampa, FL 33620
University of Southern California
Admissions, U of Southern Calif, University Pk, Los Angeles, CA 90007
Southern Illinois University, Carbondale
Dept of Anth, Southern Illinois U, Carbondale, IL 62901
Southern Illinois University, Edwardsville
Registrar, Southern Illinois U, Edwardsville, IL 62026
University of Southern Maine
Admissions, U of S Maine, Gorham, ME 04038
Southern Methodist University
Anth Dept, Southern Methodist U, Dallas, TX 75275
Southwestern at Memphis
Admissions, Southwestern at Memphis, 2000 N Pkwy, Memphis, TN 38112
Stanford University
Registrar, Stanford U, Stanford, CA 94305
Swarthmore College
Admissions, Swarthmore Coll, Swarthmore, PA 19081
Syracuse University
Grad Sch, 206 Steele Hall, Syracuse U, Syracuse, NY 13210

Temple University
Registrar, Temple U, Philadelphia, PA 19122
University of Tennessee, Knoxville
Admissions, U of Tennessee, Knoxville, TN 37916
Texas A & M University
Anth Prog, Texas A & M U, College Station, TX 77843
Texas Christian University
Admissions, Texas Christian U, Fort Worth, TX 76129
Texas Southmost College
Gene J. Paull, Texas Southmost Coll, Brownsville, TX 78520
Texas Tech University
Registrar, Texas Tech U, Lubbock, TX 79409
University of Texas, Austin
Registrar, U of Texas, Austin, TX 78712
University of Texas, Dallas
Admissions, U of Texas, Dallas, Box 688, Richardson, TX 75080
University of Texas, El Paso
Admissions, UTEP, El Paso, TX 79968
University of Texas, San Antonio
Div of Social Sciences, U of Texas, San Antonio, TX 78285
University of Toledo
Registrar, U of Toledo, Toledo, OH 43606
University of Toronto
Secy, Faculty of Arts & Sciences, Sidney Smith Hall, U of Toronto, Toronto, ON M5S 1A1, Canada
Towson State University
Admissions, Towson State U, Baltimore, MD 21204
Trent University
Dept of Anth, Trent U, Peterborough, ON K9J 7B8, Canada
Tulane University
Dean, Grad Sch, Tulane U, New Orleans, LA 70118
University of Tulsa
Dept of Anth, U Tulsa, Tulsa, OK 74104
University of Utah
Bookstore ($1.00), U of Utah, Salt Lake City, UT 84112
Vanderbilt University
Registrar, Vanderbilt U, Nashville, TN 37235
Vassar College
Office of Public Rel, Vassar Coll, Poughkeepsie, NY 12601
University of Vermont
Admissions, U of Vermont, Burlington, VT 05405
University of Victoria
Registrar, U of Victoria, Victoria BC V8W 2Y2, Canada

Virginia Commonwealth University
    Admissions, Virginia Commonwealth U, Richmond, VA 23284
Virginia Polytechnic Institute and State University
    Registrar, Virginia Polytech Inst & State U, Blacksburg, VA 24061
University of Virginia
    Admissions, Miller Hall, U of Virginia, Charlottesville, VA 22903
Wake Forest University
    Dean, Grad Sch, Box 7487, Wake Forest U, Box 7808, Reynolds Sta, Winston-Salem, NC 27109
Washburn University
    Registrar, Washburn U, Topeka, KS 66621
Washington State University
    Dean, Grad Sch, Washington State U, Pullman, WA 99164
Washington University
    Sch of Arts & Scis, Washington U, St Louis, MO 63130
University of Washington
    Registrar, Schmitz Hall, U of Washington, Seattle, WA 98195
University of Waterloo
    Registrar, U of Waterloo, Waterloo, ON N2L 3G1, Canada
Wayne State University
    Dept Secy, Dept of Anth, Wayne State U, Detroit, MI 48202
Wellesley College
    Admissions, Wellesley Coll, Wellesley, MA 02181
Wesleyan University
    Grad Office, Wesleyan U, Middletown, CT 06457
West Chester State College
    Admissions, West Chester State Coll, West Chester, PA 19380
West Georgia College
    Admissions, West Georgia Coll, Carrollton, GA 30117
West Virginia University
    Admissions & Records, West Virginia U, Morgantown, WV 26506
Western Carolina University
    Admissions, Western Carolina U, Cullowhee, NC 28723
Western Illinois University
    Registrar, Western Illinois U, Macomb, IL 61455
Western Kentucky University
    Dept of Soc & Anth, Western Kentucky U, Bowling Green, KY 42101
Western Michigan University
    Admissions, Western Michigan U, Kalamazoo, MI 49008
University of Western Ontario
    Admissions, U of Western Ontario, London, ON N6A 5C2, Canada

Western Washington University
Dept of Anth, Western Washington U, Bellingham, WA 98225
Wheaton College
Admissions & Records, Wheaton Coll, Wheaton, IL 60187
Wichita State University
Admissions, Wichita State U, Wichita, KS 67208
Wilfrid Laurier University
Registrar, Wilfrid Laurier U, Waterloo, ON N2L 3C5, Canada
College of William and Mary
Admissions, C of William and Mary, Williamsburg, VA 23185
University of Windsor
Registrar, U of Windsor, Windsor, ON N9B 3P4, Canada
University of Winnipeg
Dept of Anth, U of Winnipeg, 515 Portage Av, Winnipeg 2, MB, Canada
University of Wisconsin, Madison
Dept of Anth, 5240 Soc Sci, U of Wisconsin, Madison, WI 53706
University of Wisconsin, Milwaukee
Bulletins, U of Wisconsin, Milwaukee, WI 53201
University of Wisconsin, Oshkosh
Public Information, U of Wisconsin, Oshkosh, WI 54901
University of Wisconsin, Parkside
Public Information, U of Wisconsin, Parkside, Kenosha, WI 53140
University of Wisconsin, Whitewater
Admissions, University of Wisconsin, Whitewater, WI 53190
Wright State University
Registrar, Wright State U, Dayton, OH 45431
University of Wyoming
Admissions & Records, Box 3435, U of Wyoming, University Sta, Laramie, WY 82070
Yale University
Dept of Anth, Yale U, New Haven, CT 06520
York College of the City University of New York
Registrar, York C, CUNY, 150-14 Jamaica Av, Jamaica, NY 11451
York University
University Registrar, York U, Downsview (Toronto), ON M3J 1P3, Canada
Youngstown State University
Registrar, Youngstown State U, Youngstown, OH 44555

APPENDIX 3

MUSEUM DEPARTMENTS

American Museum of Natural History, Central Pk W at 79th St, New York, NY 10024

The Amerind Foundation, Inc., Dragoon, AZ 85609

Arizona State Museum, U of Arizona, Tucson, AZ 85721

Bernice P. Bishop Museum, 1355 Kalihi St, PO Box 19000-A, Honolulu, HI 96819

British Columbia Provincial Museum, Parliament Bldgs, Victoria, BC V8W 1A1, Canada

Museum of Anthropology, University of British Columbia, 6393 Northwest Marine Drive, Vancouver, BC V6T 1W5, Canada

Museum of Anthropology, California State University, Chico, CA 95929

Museum of Cultural History, University of California, Los Angeles, CA 90024

Carnegie Museum of Natural History, 4400 Forbes Av, Pittsburgh, PA 15213

Colorado State Museum, 1300 Broadway, Denver, CO 80203

Denver Museum of Natural History, City Park, Denver, CO 80205

Dumbarton Oaks, 1703 32nd St NW, Washington, DC 20007

Field Museum of Natural History, Roosevelt Rd & Lake Shore Dr, Chicago, IL 60605

Florida State Museum, U of Florida, Gainesville, FL 32611

Haffenreffer Museum of Anthropology, Mt Hope Grant, Bristol, RI 02809

Evelyn Payne Hatcher Museum of Anthropology, Stewart Hall, St Cloud State U, St Cloud, MN 56301

The Heard Museum, 22 E Monte Vista Rd, Phoenix, AZ 85004

Museum of the American Indian, Heye Foundation, Broadway at 155th St, New York, NY 10032

Illinois State Museum, Corner Spring & Edwards, Springfield, IL 62706

Indiana University Museum, Student Bldg 107, Bloomington, IN 47401

Museum of Anthropology, University of Kansas, Lawrence, KS 66044

Logan Museum of Anthropology, Beloit, WI 53511

Museum of Geoscience, Louisiana State University, Baton Rouge, LA 70803

Lowie Museum of Anthropology, U of California, Berkeley, CA 94720

Maxwell Museum of Anthropology, U of New Mexico, Albuquerque, NM 87131

The Museum, Michigan State University, East Lansing, MI 48824

Museum of Anthropology, University of Michigan, Ann Arbor, MI 48109

Milwaukee Public Museum, 800 W Wells St, Milwaukee, WI 53233

Museum of Anthropology, Museums Bldg, University of Missouri, Columbia, MO 65211

Nassau County Museum, Garvies Pt Mus & Preserve, Barry Dr, Glen Cove, NY 11542

National Museum of Man, National Museums of Canada, Ottawa, ON K1A OM8, Canada

University of Nebraska State Museum, 14th & U Sts, Lincoln, NE 68588

The Nevada State Museum, Capitol Complex, Carson City, NV 89710

New World Archaeological Foundation, Apartado Postal 140, Avenida 16 de Septiembre No 30, San Cristobal de Las Cassas, Chiapas, Mexico

New York State Museum and Science Service, New York State Education Bldg, Albany, NY 12234

Museum of Northern Arizona, Rt 4, Box 720, Flagstaff, AZ 86001

Anthropology Laboratories and Museum, Northern Illinois University, DeKalb, IL 60115

Ohio State Museum, Ohio Historical Society, Ohio Hist Ctr, Columbus, OH 43211

Peabody Museum, Harvard University, 11 Divinity Av, Cambridge, MA 02138

The Peabody Museum of Natural History, Yale University, New Haven, CT 06520

Peabody Museum of Salem, 161 Essex St, Salem, MA 01970

The University Museum, University of Pennsylvania, 33rd & Spruce Sts, Philadelphia, PA 19104

Provincial Museum of Alberta, Alberta Culture, 12845 102 Av, Edmonton, AB T5N 0M6, Canada

Rochester Museum and Science Center, 657 East Av, PO Box 1480, Rochester, NY 14603

Royal Ontario Museum, 100 Queen's Pk, Toronto, ON M5S 2C6, Canada

San Diego Museum of Man, 1350 El Prado, Balboa Pk, San Diego, CA 92101

Smithsonian Institution, Handbook of North American Indians, Washington, DC 20560

The Museum of Texas Tech University, PO Box 4499, Lubbock, TX 79409

The Adan E Treganza Anthropology Museum, San Francisco State University, 1600 Holloway Av, San Francisco, CA 94132

Thomas Burke Memorial Washington State Museum, University of Washington, Seattle, WA 98195

Museum of the State Historical Society of Wisconsin, 816 State St, Madison, WI 53706

INDEX

Aegean Sea, xii
Agamemnon, xii
Agogino, George, 2-3, 16
Algic Researches, 27
Allstrom, Allan, 76
Allstrom, Jane Wildesen, 76
American Anthropological Association, vi, 26
American Men and Women of Science, xiv
American Museum of Natural History, 16
American School of Classical Studies, Athens, xii, xiii
Ancient Man in North America, xiii, xiv
Anthropology
  cultural, *See* Ethnology
  definition, viii
  physical, ix
  universities offering degrees in, 150-66
Antiquities Acts, *See* Laws governing archaeology
Archaeological Handbook, xvi
Archaeologists, early women, v, viii-xiv
Archaeology
  contract, vi
  field schools, 132-49
  freelance, xvi, 125
  museum work, xvi, 56, 167-69
Archaeology (*Cont.*)
  opportunities, xv-xvii
  problems for women, v-vi, x, xiv-xv, xviii
  public, xvi-xviii
    See also Cultural resources management
  salvage, xiv, xvi, 80-1
  training, vi, ix-x, xiv-xvi
  universities offering degrees in, 150-66
Arrowhead Ruin, 33
Asia Minor, xiii

Bass, Elizabeth, 114
Benedict, Ruth, x
Bonneville Power Administration, xvi
Brew, J.O., 11
British Association of Anthropology, viii
Brockington, Donald, 119
Bronze Age, xii
Bruhns, Dan, 57-60
Bruhns, Karen Olsen, xv, 46, 51-71
  advice to teenagers, 69-71
  Belize, 69
  brother, 53
  childhood, 53-4
  Colombia, 59-64

Bruhns, Karen Olsen (*Cont.*)
  discrimination against, 56-7, 61
  dissertation, 59-60
  El Salvador, 46, 68-9
  father, 52, 54-5, 60
  field schools, 64-5
  high school, 54
  hobbies, 51
  marriage, 57-60
  Mexico, 57-8
  mother, 52, 54-5, 60
  Nicaragua, 65-7
  Peru, 65
  San Francisco State University, 51, 65
  San Jose State University, 61, 64
  teaching career, 51, 60-1, 64-5
  Thomas Weller, 51
  University of Calgary, 60-1
  University of California, Berkeley, 54-60
Bryn Mawr, xii-xiii, 8

Calico, 84-5
Camacho, Juan Armenta, 13, 15-6
Canada Council, *See* Social Sciences and Humanities Research Council of Canada
Cather, Willa, 32
Chaco Indians, 18-21
Cibola National Forest, 106-7
Cihuatan, 46
Coe, William, 106
Colorado Archaeological Society, 6
Colorado College, xiii
Columbia University, x
Coming of Age in Samoa, x
Contract archaeology, *See* Archaeology, contract
Conze, Alexander, xvii
Crete, xii, xiii
Cross, Dorothy, v
Cultural anthropology, *See* Ethnology
Cultural resources management, 76, 109
Cuzco, 65

Daugherty, Richard, 83
Death Comes for the Archbishop, 32
Denver Museum of Natural History, xiii, 7, 9
Diaz, May, 56
Dick, Herbert, 7
DuBois, Cora, x
Dunn, Edward James, 120-27
Dunn, Mary Eubanks, xvii, 113-27
  childhood, 114-5
  children, 117, 120, 122, 124, 126
  discrimination against, 124
  dissertation, 122-24
  father, 114-16
  grandfather, 114-15
  grandmother, 115
  great grandmother, 115
  high school, 116
  marriage to Edward Dunn, 120-27
  marriage to Tom Settlemyre, 117-20
  Mexico, 120
  mother, 114, 116, 122
  Peru, 122-24
  problems in career, 113-15, 124-27
  Saba, 118-19
  thesis, 119-20
  University of North Carolina, Chapel Hill, 114, 115, 116-20, 122
  Vanderbilt University, 126
Dutton, Bertha, v

Earthwatch, 70
Eastern New Mexico University, 1-3, 16
Egyptology, ix
Eisenhower, Dwight, 116
El Salvador, 46, 68-9
Engastromenos, Sophia, *See* Schliemann, Sophia
Epigrapher, 57
Escuela de Antropologia, 36
Ethnology, ix, x, 44-6, 56, 118-19
Etruscan civilization, 117-18
Eubanks, Michael, 114-16
Eubanks, Nell Bass, 114, 116, 122
Evans, Henry F., 4-5

Evolution, human, viii-ix, 28-9

Fagan, Brian M., xvii
Farmer, E. D., Scholarship, 35
Field schools, *See* Archaeology, field schools
Fogg Museum, xiii
Forest Service, *See* U.S. Forest Service
Four Corners Regional Commission, 20
Fryxell, Roald, 83

Garcia, Braulio, 12-3, 15
Goldman, Hetty, xii-xiii, xiv
Gomez, Geronimo, 14-5
Gorham, Ruth, 5
Gournia, xii
Graham, John, 57-8
Greece, xiii
Greek Treasure, The, xii
Green, Dee, 107-8
Green, Earl, 41
Green, Ernestene, xv, 76, 91-111
  childhood, 91-2
  discrimination against, 96
  dissertation, 105-6
  father, 91-2, 94, 97
  field schools, 94-6, 106-7
  Guatemala, 103-5, 106
  high school, 92-4
  hobbies, 95, 110-11
  marriage, 110-11
  mother, 92, 97
  scientific illustration, 96-7
  teaching career, 106-9
  Texas Technological College, 94-5
  Thailand, 97-101
  University of Arizona, Tucson, 95-7, 101
  University of Hawaii, 97
  University of Pennsylvania, 101-3, 106
  U.S. Forest Service, 91, 106-11
  Western Michigan University, 106-8
Green, J. Nelson, 91-2, 94, 97
Green, LaVerne, 92, 97

Hadlock, Harry, 19
Halliburton, Richard, 78
Hamen, Marsha, 47
Harvard University, x, xiii, 1, 8-11, 16, 38-40, 45, 95
Hawes, Harriet Ann Boyd, xii-xiii, xiv
Hell Gap, 16
Hills, Frances, 76-9, 81
Hissarlik, xi-xii
Holden, Frances, 30-3
Holden, Olive Price, 26-31, 32
Holden, William Curry, 26-33, 35, 39, 44
Homer, xi-xii
Hopi Indians, 5-6
Huastec Indians, 13
Hughes, Jack, 92-4

Institute of Advanced Study, xiii
Irwin, Eleanor C. Evans, 2-6, 8-9, 15, 21
Irwin, Henry T. J., 4-9, 11, 16
Irwin-Williams, Cynthia, xv, 1-23
  brother, 4-9, 11, 16
  childhood, 4-6
  Colorado Archaeological Society, 6
  commuting problems, 1-2
  discrimination against, 9-11
  dissertation, 11
  France, 10-1
  Graland School, 5
  grandfather, 4-5
  Harvard, 8-11, 16
  Hell Gap, 16
  high school, 7, 9
  Hopi Reservation, 5-6
  husband, 2, 8, 16, 21
  illness, 4
  LoDaiska, 9
  Mexico, 11-6
  mother, 2-6, 8-9, 15, 21
  Radcliffe, 8-10
  Salmon Ruin, 18-21
  teaching career, 1-3, 16, 21
Ixmiquilpan, 14

James, Alton, 19

Kavousi, xii
Kelley, David H., 25-6, 39-45, 47-8, 61
Kelley, Jane Holden, xv, 25-48, 61, 68-9
  Arrowhead Ruin, 33
  Canada, 25, 45-8
  childhood, 26-30
  children, 25-6, 41-4, 47, 69
  dissertation, 39, 41, 43-4, 46
  father, 26-33, 35, 39, 43-4
  field schools, 34-5, 39
  Harvard, 38-40, 45
  high school, 31
  husband, 25-6, 39-45, 47-8
  Ko Shari Club, 32
  Mexico, 33, 35-6
  mother, 26-31, 32
  stepmother, 30-3
  teaching career, 25-6, 40, 45-8
  Texas Technological College, 27-35, 39-43
  University of Texas, 34, 35
  Yaqui research, 44-6, 47
Kennedy, John, 116
Kenyon, Kathleen, 54
Korat Plateau, 99-101
Krieger, Alex, 36

Lambert, Marjorie, v
Laws governing archaeology, xvi-xviii, 62-3, 74-5, 109
Layard, Austen Henry, xvii
Leakey, Louis, x, 73, 85
Leakey, Mary, x, xiv
Legislation, *See* Laws governing archaeology
Linguistics, ix, 56
LoDaiska, 9
Lodge, Henry Cabot, 116
Lomayestewa, Ned, 6
Looting archaeological sites, 62-4

McGimsey, Charles R. III, xvi
Magic Mountain, 11
Mangelsdorf, Paul, 119-20, 122
Marshall, Lawrence, 7
Mead, Margaret, x
Meroe, 46
Moises, Rosalio, 44
Murray, Margaret, viii, ix, xiv
Museology, *See* Archaeology, museum work
Mycenae, xii

National Endowment for the Humanities, 20
National Historic Sites Preservation Commission, 20
National Institute of Anthropology, 12
National Museum, Thailand, 97
National Register of Historic Places, 109
National Science Foundation, 11-3, 19
National University of Mexico, 12
Navaho Indians, 20, 32
Navajuelal, *See* Tikal
Nixon, Richard, 116
Noguera, Eduardo and Mona, 33

Olsen, Verna, 52, 54-5, 60
Olsen, William, 52, 54-5, 60
Ozette, 83-4

Panhandle-Plains Historical Museum, 92-4
Pappadias, Aristides, xii
Peabody Museum, 39
Pearce, William, 33
Petrie, Sir Flinders, ix, x
Pettigrew, Rick, xvi
Pitt-Rivers, Augustus, xvii
Prehistoric Indians of the Southwest, xiii
Preservation of sites, vi, *See also* Cultural resources management
Princeton, xiii
Public Archaeology, xvi
Puebla, 13

Puleston, Dennis, 105

Quest for the Past, xvii

Radcliffe College, xiii, 8-10, 39
Richardson, Emeline, 117-18
Robles, Rudolph, 110-11
Rowe, John H., 56-60, 65

Salmon Ruin, 18-21
Salvage archaeology, *See* Archaeology, salvage
San Francisco State University, 51, 65, 81-2
San Isabel Ixtapan, 36
San Jose State University, 61, 64
Schliemann, Heinrich, xii, xviii
Schliemann, Sophia, xi-xii
Schoolcraft, Henry Rowe, 27
Sellards, E. H., 36
Settlemyre, Tom, 117-20
Shaw, Kimberly, xvi
Shinnie, Peter, 46
Smith College, xii
Social Sciences and Humanities Research Council of Canada, 46, 60, 69
Society for American Archaeology, xiv, 1, 3, 21, 26, 45-6, 87
Solheim, Wilhelm G., 97-101
Solmon, Lewis C., vi
Splendour That Was Egypt, The, ix
Stanford University, 54, 79-80
Stone, Irving, xii

Tall Candle, The, 44
Tanner, Clara Lee, v
Texas Technological College, 27-35, 39-43, 94-5
Thompson, Ray, 95-6
Tikal, 103-5, 106
Tomb of Tutankhamen, 54
Troy, xi-xii
Tulancingo, 13
Tulane University, 120-22
Turkey, xi-xii, xiii

Underhill, Ruth, x, 7
University of Arizona, 95-7, 101
University of Calgary, 25, 46-7, 60-1
University of California, Berkeley, 36-7, 54-60
University of California, Los Angeles (UCLA), 37, 60
University College, London, ix
University of Denver, x, xiii
University of Hawaii, 97
University of North Carolina, 114, 115, 116-20, 122
University of Pennsylvania, 101-3, 106
University of Texas, 34, 35
U.S. Forest Service, 73-6, 86-8, 91, 106-11

Valsequillo, 15-6
Vimbos, Archbishop Theoclitus, xi
Volk, George D., vi, xiv

Weller, Thomas, 51
Wendorf, Fred, 38, 94-5
Western Interstate Commission for Higher Education, xvi
Western Michigan University, 106-9
Wildesen, Leslie, xv, 73-88, 109
  childhood, 76-7
  field schools, 83-5
  grandmother, 76-9, 81
  guidebook, 75
  high school, 78
  hobbies, 78
  illness, 77-8
  parents, 76
  San Francisco State University, 81-3
  Stanford University, 79-80
  teaching career, 84-6
  thesis, 82

Wildesen, Leslie (*Cont.*)
University of California, Riverside, 84-6
U.S. Forest Service, 73-6, 86-8
Washington State University, 83-4
Wilkes, H. Garrison, 122
Willey, Gordon, 38
Williams, David Cary, 2, 8, 16, 21
Woolley, Leonard, 54
Wormington, H. Marie, xiii-xiv, 7-8, 9, 36

Yaqui Indians, 44-6, 47
Yugoslavia, xiii

Zapatera Island, 66-7
Zapotec Indians, 119-20, 125